Who are we?

Zicher
shlosse
enem shlissel. An einredenish
erger vi a krenk. As a laib shlof
n! Az me est chazze
fetten. Az me laig
ei'en, shlepen
chazzerim. Besser dos besteh f
gsten aider dos ergsteh f
sten. Zai schtimen vi a ka
unt. ist vu se dri
im der sh utter denk
kind iz s morgen bren
zich zorg tsh vaist
er vet sh kainer vil
nisht gloi mentsh iz d
zich alain b eder mentsh h
zein aigeneh meshegass. Vu honi
dort fligen. Vos vintsiker
gregt, iz als gezunter. V
vainiker me ret, iz als gezunte
iz
on mazel? Vos
oif der tsung. Bes
gekechts aider
chtz. Besser ain
a nei'eh tsvai. A
a feil - baideh
grois eil. A vort iz
sileh; shveigen iz vert tsvai.
shtikel mazel iz vert merer vi
ton gold. A shver hartz redt a sac

Also by Alan Kaufman

POETRY

American Cruiser

Before I Wake

Fix

Strangers Again

I Know How It Feels

FICTION

Six Stories

The End Of Time

ANTHOLOGIES

The New Generation:Fiction For Our Times
From America's Writing Programs

Horsemen Of The Apocalypse

Its The Jews: A Celebration Of New Jewish Visions

WHO ARE WE?

Alan Kaufman

DAVKA: JEWISH CULTURAL REVOLUTION
Limited Editions

 All proceeds from the sales of this book will go to *DAVKA:Jewish Cultural Revolution, Inc.*, a State-of-California non-profit organization. Published by Wordland Books, a subsidiary of *DAVKA: Jewish Cultural Revolution*. Printed in the United States of America.

First DAVKA:Jewish Cultural Revolution Limited Edition published 1997

Designed by Jill Bressler, Art Director, *DAVKA:Jewish Cultural Revolution*

Publication of this book was made possible, in part, by a grant from *The Levinson Foundation*

Library of Congress Catalog Card Number:97-69397
ISBN: 1-881822-01-X

1 2 3 4 5 6 7 8 9 0

For Diane Spencer

Table of Contents

Acknowledgements

Grateful acknowledgement is made to the following anthologies and periodicals in which these poems have appeared or are scheduled for future appearance:

"Who Are We?" in *Identity Lessons: Learning American Style: An Anthology of Contemporary Writing* edited by Maria Mazziotti Gillan and Jennifer Gillan (Penguin Books); "Bus" in *ALOUD:Voices From The Nuyorican Poets Cafe* edited by Miguel Algarin and Bob Holman (Henry Holt&Co.); "Across The Mississippi" in *Witness*; "While Now We Are Here"and "Who Are We?" in*Tikkun*; "On Reading Whitman's Song Of Myself At One O Clock In The Morning" in *Cafe Poetry Anthology* edited by June King and Larry Smith (Bottom Dog Press), *New Digressions Art and Literary Magazine, Excursus, Conjunctions;* "The Saddest Man On Earth" and "I Know How It Feels" in *Stovepiper* edited by Mike Daily (Stovepiper Books); "20/20" and "Anthem" in *Long Shot;* "Truck Stop" in *Poetry From The Exit Cafe* edited by Quentin Baker; "Chow Down Poem Food" in *Beet;* "Nancy and Frank", "I Know How It Feels" and "Relationshit" in *Wordland Dossiers #2* with Harold Norse and Bucky Sinister; "Monday Afternoon in Haight Ashbury" and "In A Window Dark Night" in *McGill Street;* "I Don't Want To Be With Woman" in *Awaa-te;* "Anonymous" in *Bull Horn;* "Kuwait" in *National Poetry Magazine Of The Lower East Side* and *HOWL;* "Let Us" in *HOWL;* "Java Man" in *Bouillabaisse;* "The Time I Drew Angels" in *DAVKA:Jewish Cultural Revolution;* "She" in Pink Pages.

The following poems have appeared abroad in translation: "Who Are We?"and "On Reading Whitman's Song Of Myself At One O Clock In The Morning" translated into Swedish by Carl-Johan Vallgren appeared in *Bonniers Litterara Magasin* (Stockholm, Sweden); "Nancy and Frank" and "I Don't Want To Be With Woman" translated into Swedish by Carl-Johan Vallgren appeared in *Pequod* (Malmo, Sweden); "Nancy Reagan and Frank Sinatra", "Alien", "I Know How It Feels", "Stud Of The Apocalypse" translated into German by Bert Papenfus appeared in *SLAM! Heftige Dichtung Aus Amerika* (Edition Druckhaus, Druckhaus Galrev, Berlin, Germany); "The Last Emphysema Gasp Of The Marlboro Man" translated into German by Sasha Anderson and "Kuwait" translated into German by Stefan Doring appeared *AM LIT Neue Literatur Aus Den USA* edited by Gerhard Falkner and Sylvere Lotringer (Druckhaus Galrev, Edition Druckhaus, Berlin, Germany); "Across The Mississippi" and "The Saddest Man On Earth" translated into German by Andreas Koziol appeared in *Chelsea Hotel: A Magazine of the Arts* (Freiburg, Germany)

I wish to give thanks to the following people for their love, counsel, devotion, friendship, inspiration and assistance: Diane Spencer, Isadora Kaufman, Meenoo Yashar, Jill Bressler, Emerald O'Leary, Michael Rudder David Shelonko, Naomi Fiss, Julian Levinson, Helen and Angelo Freda, David Carlson, Jeff Clinton, Joe Herlicy, Christopher Doyle, Michael Rudder, Hersch Silverman, Mark Smith, Lowell Nobel, Carl Little Crow, Carl Johan-Vallgren, Thomas Wohlfahrt, Dr. Henry Kaminer, Josh Kun, Michal Friedlander, Rabbi Jack Frankel, Penina Perl, Norman, Mark Gottlieb, Rosa, Walter, Danny Shot

In Memorium: David Lerner (1951-1997), fellow poet, editor and friend.

Every good artist paints what
he is

Jackson Pollack

My life was never so

precious

to me as now

James Wright

And Abram went down to Egypt

(Genesis 12:10)

I come not to bury poetry but to blow
it up

David Lerner

PART ONE: American Cruiser

BUS

At the gateway
to America
Greyhound strikers
shrieked:
"You won't
get out!"

Ninety bucks
to cross the
land by bus

For this, embarked,
anonymous. neither
lonely or glad,

a young man
with family
stared at his
ticket, afraid

and an old aunt
stooped to her
bags as a skinhead
cursed her back

and a punk with a pierced nose
sighed: " this country's
fucked"

and beside me
an ex-con, patting
his hair, snapped:
"Man, I done my time!
I'm going home"

We boarded like
souls on Charon's bark

As the road
stroked by wheels
removed its dress,

one by one
we laid our tired
heads on breasts
of trembling
glass

But somewhere
in Pennsylvania
I woke,
my face a gun

HOUSE OF STRANGERS

Her face,
cut from patient
ebony, looked ill

A trash bag
of belongings
rode her lap

I guessed her
life had been
a suicide of kindness
repaid in grief

And somewhere in Cheyenne
I asked where she was going

and she said that she
was going to the
House of Strangers
in Reno, Nevada
where God sits in a
clapboard casino
playing the one-armed bandit

"Heaven is a hotel,"
she smiled, "and if you meet
His price, the Big Guy
will let you sit

and listen to the wind
blow: Whooooooo!'
and I knew
she was crazy

"My daughter-in-law
swore I'd die, but
it's good exercise
for me to ride. Look
at me, am I dead?"
And I knew
that she was

I laughed. "You look,"
I said "like morning
in Atlanta"

She grinned and
wrapped my hand
in a glove of bone

"Is it a way still?"
"Not far. We're
getting there"
"Good," she sighed,
"I'm ready"

She showed me a bag
big with silver dollars:
"Ten years of my life
there," she laughed

And later, while she slept,
I stole a few
to feed myself

A SCREAM FROM THE BOTTOM

Across the Continental Divide
the bus climbed
to the frontier of Montana
to the highest point
on earth
that most of us
had ever seen

Along the prairie fence
wild antelope fled
the shadow of the slums
and drought farms
and crack belts and prisons
we'd brought with us

Among us sat an ex-con
wearing a shower cap
to protect his oily
natural. He said
the antelope were deer,
and an out-of-work Union
Pacific man who'd boarded
in Larimer
shook his head
in mock despair
and told him what
they were

The ex-con listened, awed,
and asked: "But don't dey
got deer in Home, Home
On Da Range?" The Union Pacific
Man nodded. "But not
around here."

Further on, a bleach blonde
who'd claimed to be
a university lecturer
in English lit
whirled in a violent
commotion of sequins,

exclaiming that she'd just
seen something white as the moon
and tall as a man perched
on that distant hill,
and the railroad man
chuckled: "Maybe it was
a white stallion,"
which is impossible,
he confided, leaning
my way, "You won't
find any around these
parts. Marlboro killed
the last one, shooting
a commercial. Chased it
with a copter and
it fell to the dust
with a broken neck.
Read about it in
the newspaper"

Still, he let her
think that's what
she'd seen. "Why
add to her misery,"
he winked

The other passengers
seemed not to care
The Sacramento-bound
Soviet emigres still
nibbled the sandwiches
they'd passed among
themselves outside
the Arbys rest stop
in Cheyenne
Babies slept on laps
and shoulders. A clean-
shaven traveling salesman
with a new haircut and a
face like a side of raw bacon
read with moving lips
in his Bible

"Mormon," spat a grey-
beard veteran of the
Tet offensive. Earlier,
he'd told us his story
of thrusting a 45. against
the ribs of a suspected V.C.,
only to have it misfire
and blow off three of his
fingers. He reached under
his seat and produced the
fifth he'd been working on
since Des Moines

As it passed between our
smoke-filled mouths, fading
daylight turned the whiskey
bronze

Night seemed to fall
just as the last drop
fell on to the
vet's tongue

He tossed the bottle
to the floor, it struck
loudly, and the eyes of
the scab driver looked
up, but the vet stared
back, masked by the shadow
of his cap's peaked brim,
and his eyes contained
the death which we had
cringed from in our cribs
and criminally ambitious
cities, the death which
as a soldier
he had borne away from
our downcast bedrooms and
grave-kitchens and spread
to a foreign war in our names,
and that death had come home

to find us, and we joined

with his defiance,
a legion of memory,
our heads in silhouetted ranks,
our eyes a scream
from the bottom of silence,
and the driver's stare
regained the road,
remained there.

As the high ground of America
passed unseen beneath our wheels
darkness filled the sky,
turned our windows to mirrors
And there was nothing to do,
nothing to see, nothing to say

There was only our sleepless
faces waiting to arrive

TRUCK STOP

Shining like a silver dollar in the sun, the Greyhound American Cruiser drew up at one of those fold-out postcard eating joints where rig drivers in Stetson hats bang the pinball home with the heels of their hands and posters of missing children hang on the wall. Hydraulic brakes hissed as the wheels slowed and the door folded back like an accordion, and one by one the passengers got off and looked around, wondering where they were.

The riggers watched them file in, with looks hard as whetting stones, but their eyes sharpened knives when a string of long hairs dressed in God and country-defiling clothes shuffled through the door, including a very pregnant wisp of a girl with a face like moonlight and wearing Old Glory for a shawl. One of these, a skinny tattooed boy with silver earrings in his lobes and nose and lips, and his head bound in a calico bandana, headed for the games, and the riggers let him through, then closed around him with latent violence as his quarters clunked loudly in the slot.

The boy played better than good. He worked the bumpers and the ball like a brisk dance and when he was done the score was gonging five alarms and he had won everything, which came to points. And one of the riggers leaned close to the boy and asked, respectfully, where he was headed.

He produced his last cigarette from a crumpled pack, slipped it to his lips, slid his weight from one torn sneaker to the other, and a match flared. "Cal'fornia," he said, splitting the name in two, and all the riggers nodded like a team. They had seen his like passing through before. They knew he had no family there.

"Gonna deal crack and fuck your brains out, won't you"
sneered one
rigger.

"Pot, maybe," said the boy, "I need cash bad. I got a kid on the way," then smiled coolly at his girl. "She's almost due."

She was there among them, quiet as a moonbeam, and the startled riggers turned up their sunbeaten faces in sly grins and mumbled, "Hi." It was hard not to stare. One of them offered gently: "The barbecue beef is real good here," and looked at the road. "Best eat up. Not another stop in Nebraska for a hundred miles." "I know," she smiled wanly, "I just feel too sick to eat."

But by her famished face the riggers knew it wasn't so, that the kids were broke, and that the boy had spent their last change to play. Angrily, one of the riggers broke off and returned with a bag of sour lemon balls. "My wife," he said, "sucks them when she's got somethin' in the oven." The girl received his offering without a word. And just then the bus driver announced it's time to board.

"Well," said the boy, encircling her shoulder.

The riggers watched as the big silver cruiser sped away, and didn't move or say anything until one of them broke in cheerfully with: "Hell, they're young. They'll find some

place to live as soon as they arrive."
"Sure," snarled the one who'd bought candy. "And I bet they spend their nights in the gutter, and that baby gets dropped in some squatters hole somewhere, like a god damn animal."

The riggers absorbed the sober truth of it. And the one who spoke bit his lip that he had not done something more, but he saw so many like them passing through, and there was no helping it, no helping it at all.

LET US

Let us
take ourselves aboard a bus
and travel to the dispossessed
and let us praise their dreamless eyes and hardened smiles
with rogue words of truth
in the killing fields of their hopes
the slum wards and ragged towns and stolen farms

Let us
take to them the carnival
of our mad and scattered lives

Let us bring them the mountain
Let us give them the vision
of an open window, an unlocked door, a bed to sleep in, a plate of food

Let us give
them the keys to the house of their love
Let us bare our throats tattooed with roses
our breasts sequined with diamonds
our loins hot with dragons
our hands and feet pierced with beauty

Let us come
to their dusty squares and drinking holes
with canticles of magnificent defeat
Let us deliver in their mangers

of pollution and penitentiaries, shopping malls and tenements
the hard, beautiful birth of the heart

Let us bring renewal
Let us declare the death of despondency and tyrants

For I have seen our campfires pitched beside the roads
like fallen, still-burning miraculous stars
I have seen our bus voyaging to innocence

I have seen us poet-dogs tossed
the last decade of this century, like a bone,
after ninety years of science and war,
reason and corporation, art and Auschwitz

I have seen my vocation descend like a pen
to a page that can never be filled with enough truth
I have crossed a continent of despair
with a summons much older than lies,
and I swear to you, Poets,
I live for greater than myself

You
street-latin Elizabethan hustlers,
I tell you time has come to deal death's passionate kiss to kings
Time has come to bare our asses in Paradise
Time has come to strip for freedom
Time has come slut dogs, drag queens,
sadomasochists and criminals
to be Tom Paines, Franklins and Jeffersons

Time has come to write
the Constitution
with our poetry and flesh

Time has come
to costume up for Liberty and ride
with words like steel-tipped whips
into the soul of America
and rage there and sing

till mouth of every starving child
is fed

ON READING WHITMAN'S SONG OF MYSELF AT ONE O'CLOCK IN THE MORNING

An image or two stuck:
the swimmer tossed into the sea and surfacing
with damp curls, reborn, beside himself with joy,
and further on you enjoin the student,
me I guess,
to destroy you, the teacher,
and that will spread your breast

BANG!
You're dead

I'm out here, Walt, rushing broke
down Mission to beg Unemployment
to cut me a check
I'm out here in dry dock,
spilling my guts like a dweeb to a bunch of drunks
whose names I don't know,
and I'm thinking I'll have these narratives
from Hell tattooed on my skin,
so I can step up to cops,
rip off my shirt
and shout: Read this!

Because underfoot, Walt,
is not grass but flames
I'm living the private American inferno
where anguish is something you do at home,
behind locked doors; terror
expressed to strangers in rented rooms
anonymously, and late at night
over telephones to friends, who sob in turn
of their own HIVs of incurable hepatitis
enlarged livers secreting
schizophrenic genes of utter emotional
drear, shame success tumors,
and harrowing despair at the ghosts

of their walking fathers

I am laughing by kitchen light, Walt,
bent with rot-toothed
grin over your most famous poem,
watching my reflection
in the night of ashtray eyes
and lips shaped by the vowel of Oblivion,
and tonight, Walt, I am James Dean
on the day of his death,
I am Marilyn Monroe's baby grown,
the second one she lost,
and all that I have been
is falling down
like a house of cards
in this room by-the-week,
with my iodine-dabbed
gangrenous leg like a seated shriek
I am shrieking, Walt, for a drink,
for a fix, for a mother, for a God,
for a kindness, for a child,
for a prayer I can say
without sneering in my guts

I'm asking, Walt,
have you got like me
slant eyes, hook nose,
black skin and Spanish lips,
do they let my type with dick,
one ball, big tits, mascara, wig,
pumps, two wombs
and cocktail dress into Heaven?

I'm, sick of Wonder bread, Walt
Have you got democratic steak for me?
Have you got red-blooded boneless
shoes for me, without holes, a lot
of ketchup, size twelve?
Because I'm years in the alleys
in the garbage cans in the rain
laying for you with a poem like a gun
I don't know what's got into me
I'm trigger obsessed

Must be the Bronx where I grew up
Must be Bronx make me
hard as an aerial snapped
off a car, as a packed
Saturday night special,
and I wanna rumble,
Walt, I wanna mix it up

I'm infected with the virus of the poor
who never read the Norton Anthology of Modern Verse
Who sing madrigals of bucked teeth,
harelip and rickets, recite sonnets
of executed eviction summonses
for unpaid back rents, and job
applications to Macdonalds,
and critically deconstruct
stab wounds painted with Mercurochrome

I've got a vision, Walt, of savage
love for the one-eyed drunk,
the limping thief, the unshaven
cabby in drag
I've got a vision, Walt
of the cosmic benefit
of sound nutrition
of medical attention
of housing and of voice
in a truly democratic society
on the filthy piles of flesh
dying on the pavement
I've got a vision of extended hand
of lifting arm
of healing souls leafing and loafing
in winter coats and resoled shoes
and of their lonely power to destroy you,
once and for all, old teacher,
and spread your breast a billion-fold,
to absurd bursting point, like gout,
and not just your breast, old fella,
but your neck and cheeks,
guts and buttocks and knees
will swell, inflamed with their angry joy

And the poor will not drown in the sea
Their deaths, for too long
given over to God, will return to us
with restored trust
in the thriving intimacy of the earth
and from love we will come
and with love we will see
even in the hour of our greatest blindness
that to an even gentler love we go

WHO ARE WE?

Into the past
I go like a stranger
to discover why at night
I lay alone as a child
waiting for the front door
to slam, my father gone
to night-shift work,
and my mother, Marie, to enter,
unable to sleep, and tell me
tales of childhood
war, pursued by those
who, as she spoke,
seemed to enter the room,
Gestapo men in leather coats
who ordered me to pack
and descend to a waiting truck,
for I am still going to Auschwitz
though a grown man in 1995
I am still boarding the freight,
crushed against numbed, frightened
Jews and Gypsies and Russian
soldiers and homosexuals
crossing frontiers to be gassed

I am her, in my heart,
though I am six feet two
and two hundred and ten pounds
and have played college football
and served as a soldier
and have scars from fights

with knives and jagged
bottles smashed on bars

I am still her, little girl,
hiding in chicken coops
and forests, asleep on dynamite
among partisans
I am still her, brushing teeth
with ashes
from the ruins of nations
gutted in war

I am still her brown eyes
and black hair of persecution
foraging scraps of thistle soup,
a star-shaped patch
sewn to my shirt

I am still my mother
every day in the streets
of New York or San Francisco,
the chimney skies glow and swirl
with soot like night above
a crematorium, or the Bronx
incinerator chute where I
threw out trash in a brick
darkness shooting sparks

I am still her in the streets
of Berkeley, walking among
sparechangers, dyed-hair punkers,
gays in stud leather, Blacks,
Mexicans and Asians

I am still her rounded up
among poets and thieves
and politically incorrect
social deviants
on sun-drenched sidewalks
in the Mission and the Haight,
Greenwich Village, the Lower
East Side, or anywhere the weird
congregate in tolerance

And every day in this age
of intolerance,
in a mental ghetto
affirmed by the homeless,
I pass the dying
with the loud ring of my boots,
ashamed to think that perhaps
my heels are the last thing
they heard
Every day I am a
survivor of AIDS and poverty

Every day I sit in cafes
watching tattoos turn to numbers
and I grow angry
I want America back
I want America to be
the home I never had

And you, who are you
if you hear my voice?
Who are you, stranger
if you read these words?

Who are we
who stand threatened
in these times of darkness?
Who are we, condemned to die,
who do not know ourselves
at all?

ACROSS THE MISSISSIPPI

We crossed the Mississippi's muddy brown expanse in a blinding thunderstorm,
creeping over a big suspension bridge whose name nobody knew,
in a bus with sheets of rain battering windows feeble as eyelids
trembling in fear,
and we could hardly see but for glimpses of suspension cable over
the sullen river, on the banks houses like garbage cans with pedal lids,
and over it all a sky the color and consistency of clay,

with an occasional lightening bolt seaming it like a cheek
wrinkled in angry laughter.
And we didn't even know that we were crossing
the Mississippi until that bottle of Fleishman's whiskey
fell from the overhead luggage rack
and the lanky driver with hair in his eyes, and rolled sleeves,
and a pack of filterless Pall Malls
cast a glaring boozy eye our way in the rear view mirror,
pulled over the bus right there on the bridge
and announced for the twentieth time since leaving New York City
that Federal regulations prohibit booze consumption aboard,
which hadn't made a goddamned difference to anyone
for over a thousand miles so far,
and didn't make a goddamned difference now.
The drunkards still snuck drinks and the sober people didn't.
And he put the bus into high gear and gunned it.
And this was as we crossed the Mississippi,
though we didn't even know it.

Assumed it was just some trash river,
as some birds are trash birds — say, the robin.
A trash river, some of us thinking, a love canal,
an above-ground industrial sewer of radioactive Republican by-products
by which to contaminate and kill the poor on the merry road to profit.
So we didn't even know that we we were crossing that famous river,
had no way to know.
Most of us had never seen it.
I had come from a transient hotel room east of the Hudson to find
my gain in California. I didn't have much money.
When the bus pulled into a rest stop, I stayed on board — didn't
stumble off like the others blear-eyed drunk on lack of sleep
to gorge myself on fast food.
I was making it across the continent on three loaves of wonder bread
and two jars of peanut butter and one of jam, and so far so good.
And that bottle of Fleishman's that dropped out missed
a passenger's big pink ear by a hair's breadth, bounced
without shattering, and rolled to a stop against the bolted leg of a chair,
and the passenger, his name as I recall was Chopper,
reached down, retrieved the bottle, held it up with a big grin
and while everybody in the back of the bus roared with approval,
he waved it at the driver, who stopped the bus and made the speech.
And then, after a moment's sullen pause,
suddenly the driver's voice came on again, but kinder,

and he said with a gentle pride that surprised most of us I think:
"You are crossing the Mississippi River, on the Sasquahana
Bridge, and are about to enter the town of Shilo Springs."
And the effect on us of this announcement was like what maybe the Hebrews felt when Moses told them after all their wanderings
and afflictions: *You are crossing the Jordan River. You are entering the Promised Land.*
Because everyone became very serene suddenly,
and reposed quiet in their seats,
some with heads cocked, and just slow-watching the passage
occur.

The ex-con wearing the shower cap, the hungry computer jock,
the professional piercer with earrings in his eyes and ears and exposed nipples in a fishnet shirt,
the old woman with a garbage bag containing all her
possessions riding on her lap,
the Nam vet with a baseball cap gray beard blue eyes
the color of anti-freeze,
that girl who looked like every girl I'd ever seen writhe nude
in the glaring footlights of a topless bar,
the silent man who refused our repeated offers
of whiskey with a tight, unresentful smile,
and even the loud, hard-muscled mustached guy
with a face like a skinned and butchered leg of steer
and who claimed to be a lumberjack
(but whom many of us figured for a killer of some kind,
in flight from his latest barroom manslaughter),
everybody, and that includes that stiff and uncommunicative
respectably-dressed middle-aged lady
with silver hair who shuddered when asked by the ex-con
for a match, everyone without exception
seemed to give up their tension and their fear
like the dying surrender of a soul on its way to final rest
and we sat back and just let the transition occur.

And on the other side of the Mississippi River it was like an older,
more innocent time in America.
There was a kind of canal branching from the main body of water,
and less turbulence to the rain
and we could see clearly through the windows
as an old time boat paddled its way to the interior
past banks lined with weeping willows,

and the houses were bigger than they'd seemed from the bridge,
they were stately gray with age
and big columns announced their facades
and dark mandala-shaped stained glass attic windows,
the kind you see in pictures in magazines,
suggested, at least to my mind, the sanctuary and safety
of a family cemetery vault, of time and place and the dignity
of knowing where you come from and where you'll probably end up too.
And this calmed me, calmed everyone I think,
and then the bus met, to our delight, a roadblock
and we had to detour through little old time streets
and it was peaceful for a few brief minutes,
and then the bus drew up to the edge of a puddle
as wide and deep as a stream
and the brakes hissed and the driver's voice announced:
"We are going to ford this puddle," and we cheered.
And just then a man dressed in a green flannel shirt and denim
coveralls stepped from the door of one of the houses
and stood there stock still on the porch to watch.
The rain had lessened and as the bus descended,
almost kissing the rim of the tires,
we watched the man's face watching us
with a kind of compassionate interest, as if encouraging our
success, and when the bus climbed out on the other side
dripping like a baptized bather
the driver braked again.
"We'll sit here a minute," he said "to let the brakes dry."
And that man on the porch,
I guess he saw our faces dim in the tinted rain swept-windows,
and lifted his hand in a wave.
A few of us waved back,
and he beamed a smile. Then he turned and entered the house.
We heard the porch door slam,
crisp and clean in the pattering rainfall.

KUWAIT

I feel good
Do you feel good?
This morning, jets zapped me too fast to
   catch their model and make
   I'm all shot up

Tonight, tanks broke my neck
The dunes shriek and moan
to cum in dying boys with rolling eyes
  and impact sucks off Scuds with spewing heads
  in streets of cringing kids
but on I go, joyous, George and Saddam,
  to liberate the holy shrines
  of Exxon and Islam

I am enraged afraid in my trench of jackals
  baring grins at searchlight moons
I had never seen in Kansas
  tracers stitch the night's black coat
  or so many bellies split like dropped
    shopping bags
so many thoughts blown
  like sand from the mind
so many footprints tracked like ants
  to the nuclear picnic
so many smiling chests, bullet-
  kissed with blood

I feel good
Do you feel good?
It's good to die in war to lie spitting
  guts and gazing down at ankle-
    severed boots
Remember me when you pay the gas pump
You'll think, counting your change:
  Why, that cost ten cents less than last week
and as you pull away
you'll see my phantom wave friendly
in camouflage fatigues and hear
  the register ring *Semper Fi*
that I enabled you to take
  your mistress out
and drop your wife off
  at church
and ferry your son to
  his football game
all without walking
I gave you gas to cruise the Tenderloin
  on your night out, bargain with whores,

a percentage of whose fee I paid for
in blood

But don't cry for me
I lived, I saw T.V.
Had my tonsils and appendix pulled
Cracked the books and passed my tests
Saw all the *Honeymooner* reruns
a hundred times
Broke my jaw canoeing on Lake Tahoe
Jerked off in bathroom stalls at school
There were just so many visits to MacDonalds
left in me
I could never have afforded that Honda
anyway
I did my skateboarding
I got under bras
I fingered holes
I had never been abroad
They cut your head off here
for drinking booze
and by the time we took the streets back
all the veiled girls were gone

But don't mourn for me
Look at the nice frame they put my picture in,
posed in parade dress behind
a nailed-up flag
and my mother presses lips
to my Kodak Color cheeks
and my sister makes
such a legend of me
that her dates dump her
for chicks who worship sex
more than ghosts
and Pensacola is the same
Trenton flows on unchanged
Minnesota is still fucking cold
Soon the World Series
Soon the Superbowl
Soon the NBA playoffs
Soon new elections
I'm glad we repelled the invader

The invader is glad he repelled us
Goodbye flotilla of international destroyers
The tankers roll once more
The refineries are belching
The oil is gushing
Onward flow black crude
Onward vital stuff of speedometers
Onward mad angelic nectar of hidden radar,
breath tests and hit-and-run
Onward, go, go, go manic adrenalin
of Neal Cassidy roads
restored to billboard health
for motel saints
with nukes and bazooks
and copters and stealths

Long will Kuwait live in the annals
of our oil-heated stoves
You will sing of our sacrifice
at the Indy Five Hundred
and when 16 cylinder monster roadsters
spew flames at National Speedway
You will place caps over your hearts
to think of us in Chevrolet dealerships
and used car lots
Our courage will purr in your
Meineke mufflers
You'll bless us in Montana wastes
when your plugs spark
When cavalcades of limos bear to graves
your well-fed hearts
for heavenly registration
on wings of license plates

AMERICAN CRUISER

It is a thirty-six passenger bus
A tarnished silver bullet
shot from the barrel of the past
Anybody can afford to board it
so only the poor do, the fugitive, the lost

The rest fly
The ones with credit cards, homes and jobs,
friends and telephones and no time
for the long, lonely roads of America

It does not carry those
who will not trust
to sit beside a stranger in ragged clothes,
who cannot endure a sufferer too long,
those ragamuffin clowns and tattered acrobats
who work the medicine shows and freak stalls
around the American big top

Once I flew above the ranges and mountains,
the gas pump towns and speed traps
where lives burn like ignited fuel
with heat and stink and smoke

Once, I pushed the button on my seat,
reclined and gazed through a porthole
at space as thin, blue and unlivable
as my soul

I descended to my appointments drunk
but it was not just booze that sent me crashing
through the tent
I fell to see the land below,
beneath the belly of the plane,
the gameboard where fires burn ignored

I fell to be reborn from
the belly of a bus

And at first the gloom and boredom
of the trip was a punishment
At first each mile was a year

My pride rebelled against
this crapgame of ravaged character
this savage speeding palace of bad luck

But then I looked into the eyes
of those around me

and they stared back with hunger-
pitched hankering in supermarket aisles,
with the guilt of unmanicured fingers
trailed larcenous along
the rusted rim of bargain basement bins

Their eyes gave back irises cracked
and dulled by unobtainable shoes
and even before I saw clear through to the
psyches behind them (tracked like
needle arms, running with shame sores
and wounds of woodgrain alcohol)
their eyes glowed with the uncontrolled
horizontal roll of broken black
and white T.V.'s

We barreled along at the speed limit
encased in tons of tired metal
on threadworn tires
to destinations as unknown
to us as the dust
on Mars

We were fugitive
past houses with big deep dish satellite
antennas and shiny economy cars
parked in garages
We peered, friendless,
at steam-ironed people in pastel-colored
summer clothes, gathered on lawns,
with cocktail heads leaned close in gossip

We peered envious
at soap-scrubbed families leaving
storybook churches for baseball
picnics of chicken and potato salad

We saw our own reflections
pass in shop windows as
we sped through Steven Spielberg
suburbs where lovable, good-natured
aliens with glowing fingers can land
unharmed and share a child's bedroom

but where cops would check our I.D.'s

and throw us into lock-up for vagrancy
if we didn't keep
going, so we kept on going,
and our heads sunk sad
against the dying day
burnishing the windowpanes

I had time to think
and unrelenting locomotion

I had the names of towns to remember:
Smith Mills, Belle Fontaine, Graysport,
Grabell, Liverett, Cascilla Junction,
Johnsonville, Sharky, Black Bayou, and
Saints Rest

I had steel mills in Pittsburgh
Fairways in Bloomington
Endless fields of Des Moines
Praries stitched with abandoned stagecoach trials
around Larimer
Simulated Wild West gunfights in Butte
A million-to-onw shot on a one
hour stopover in Reno

I had the old forties-make silver
colored Airstream bus parked
on rusted rims behind an Arbys
in Salt Lake City, that I swore
someday to come back and buy

I had all that and sixty dollars
rolled in a tight wad secured
by a rubber band in my jeans pocket

And I had the moment I woke
somewhere on the California borderline
at daybreak
Around me lay
cowhide-colored hills furred with heather
and dimly outlined grazing cows

and the Pacific sky chasing the night
all the way to Asia
I drew myself upright in my seat
to collect myself for the ever-
nearing end of the ride
and as I had never known on other days,
I had the morning

JUST SO LONG

If I will write as a nurse
performs in a hospital emergency,
attend to truth as to a gunshot wound,
a crack addiction shackled howling
to a bench, an asthmatic attack,
a drunk bleeding from the head —

If I will establish with you,
my audience, the sort of trust,
based on desperate faith, of a cabby
driving strangers garbed in shadow
to a midnight street of the East Bronx —

If I will provide you the same relief
given terminal cancer patients
by visiting clowns, film stars
and first ladies —

then angels in Paradise
will slap my shoulder and offer
to light my cigarette
        but I'll refuse

and the angels, crowding in, will say,
like tough, warm-hearted waitresses:
    Honey, take it while you can get it
        and still I will refuse

I will say: *Give me to safeguard*
the light within you
Give me the fire that consumes you
I will be your poet

I will keep the flame
though unconsumed by it

And you, you must judge me
not only by my words
but by my qualities as a man

I will build each poem
from your frailty

I will erect soaring arches
from ribcages of the homeless
I will buttress the topmost
spire, not with fiercesome
gargoyles, but with a nurse,
a plumber, a short order cook,
a housing project custodian

I will place behind the altar
a trio of recovering substance abusers:
a manic depressive vet,
a tattooed biker,
a bank robber,
holding hands in a circle,
heads bowed in prayer

These will be your messiahs

These, and in a domed
stained glass manger
an infant crack-addicted
born begging relief in an incubation
chamber,
attended by a harried nurse, the grim
set of her jaw,
under the star emblem
of a county squad car

And just so long
as I have noted
the haggard faces, the lips
sick of talking, the ears bleeding
lies

Just so long
as I have caught
arthritis-crippled hands
hair limp and lusterless,
stubbled cheeks deprived of razors,
the hairnets and rotting rubberbands
and street-scarred, laceless
shoes of our lives

Just so long as I have
traveled Highway 80 down an
endless Appian Way, where
the poor hang from crosses
pierced by a thousand points
of light

Just so long as I have
portrayed the rich who fly
above, like Gods, in jets
and do not hear the rage
below of those rejecting
martyrdom but nailed up
anyway

Then within me will spring,
murderous, a poet's flow,
from prison yards and crack dens
and stolen cars,
a blood river coursing
past factory towns and inner cities
where life shut down and
left the years to waste
on weed curbs and in death canals

A poet's voice roaring,
overflowing, hammering down
the dikes and dams of
spiritual cowardice

and I will be whole
though broke, hungry,
kicking alcohol

I will be whole
though fugitive on earth
and I will climb
past divorce, a lost daughter,
the skull cracked in a
barroom brawl, the spine
shattered by a drunken spill
down stairs,
the scarred wrists of suicide

I will be whole and I will climb
the last hill to home

PART TWO: Jewz

20/20

As usual Norman the retired Dentist
is driving us all to *shul:*
Me in the front seat of his *BMW,*
sad-eyed Rosa in back
with her tattooed arm
and deliciously mysterious smile.
And on a Saturday like this
as we drive through the Richmond
District of San Francisco
with the indigo sky trembling
like a tincture of blue
on a laboratory slide
its hard to imagine that
the notorious Doctor Josef Mengele,
Auschwitz's Angel of Death,
once used Rosa for a human guinea
pig because of her blue eyes
or that Norman, so lively, brusque
and friendly, is dying of prostrate cancer.
Allright, never mind, its a beautiful day.
And so now, we stop to
pick up Shirley, all 91 years of her,
kina hora, may she live to be a hundred
and twenty, but: where is she?
We peer into the dark space of her opened
garage. "She's sitting in
her car I bet, to keep warm" guesses
Norman, and sure enough, outlined against
her windshield her feathery white hair appears
and from the cars abruptly opened door
an orthopedic shoe touches earth,
then another, and she is hobbling
quickly towards us, clutching her famous
hand bag, the one with her name SHIRLEY
repeated endlessly across the front:
'So dat I can't forget my name
and needer should YOU!'

With suave grace I slip out and
open for her the door. She refuses help
into her seat but looks up with her

slanted red mouth like an ironically
placed comma and says: "Tank you honey!"
And we're off again, and as usual
someone asks: Did anyone see twenty twenty
last night?"

"You mean" says Rosa "About the Frenchman was
married to Japanese woman turned out was
a man, and had a baby by her? Or Him? It was so
confusing!"

"Can you believe that idiot!?" growls Norman "Of all
the stupid people in the world! And he was a
diplomat to boot!"

"Oh" says Shirley "That I didn't mind so much.
But what did you think the story of that woman
what cut off her husband's penis?"

How impoverished I feel, who, from principled
cultural pride refuses to own a television
or watch such programs. Instead,
at home with classical music turned up high
I compose sterile empty poems about how moths
immolating themselves on light bulbs are
like poets drawn ineffably to death
as though it were a light."

But just see what I'm missing:

"Yes" Rosa agrees "That was a crazy story but the Frenchman
having baby with Japanese man was craziest story
I ever heard. "

"How could he not know?" I gasp shyly.

"That's the point" says Rosa "The Japanese man had his genitals
removed and he had some way of tucking his penis into
the hole where his scrotum used to be..."

I dare not even turn around to look her in the eyes as she speaks
of such things; I'm blushing from ear to ear,
me the hot shot radical underground poet who prides himself

upon his association with shadowy subterraneans of the counterculture:

"Uh huh" I say nervously, "Uh huh" as we sail beneath a canopy of trees.

"Yes" says Rosa with an air of exquisite European refinement "So when they made love the Frenchman could not tell the difference. He must have been a virgin. And even then I wonder in this day and age with so much sex lib how he could not know the difference."

"He was an idiot!" snaps Shirley

"Stupidest human being I ever saw!" roars Norman

"Yes" says Rosa "I agree. But it was all a trick the Japanese man played. He had a baby by another marriage with a woman, and so one day he told the Frenchman: 'Here. I gave birth to your son.' And the Frenchman bought it."

I nearly beat my head on the dashboard for the sheer stupidity of the Frenchman. "And where's the Japanese man now?" I demanded to know.

"Divorced" said Rosa"Dancing and singing in the chorus of Madame Butterfly" and she said it as though this were the most perfectly logical outcome in the world.

And as I glanced at the numbers on her arm tattooed
at Auschwitz, suddenly it all *was* logical, as one by
one the numerals seemed to rise from her skin,
expand, grow wings, lift off like butterflies
and flutter out the window
into the sabbath afternoon.

WHILE NOW WE ARE HERE

At the cemetary seven of us took hold of his casket.
The chapel official waved off Rabbi Jack.
"Only six carry" he said "You pray".
But Rabbi Jack shrugged him off, said:
"I promised I'd walk with Robert to the end",
and my heart ached with gladness for his answer.

With his pocket-sized
prayer book held up he led us,
his other hand firmly
on the casket,
an explorer, first in the prow of his ship,
reaching undiscovered shores.

Up ahead beefy grave diggers with snide
grins straddled the hole.
But the prow of his prayer
cleaved them as froth.
Our solemn assembly filled the place.
From the warm timbre of his voice
arose a shul under blustery sky,
where some could weep
and others rise to the meaning of death.

As our shovels tossed dirt,
we made Robert seperate from us
so that we could keep him forever.
After Kaddish was read,
we formed two lines
for his widow Sarah to pass through.
With an encircling arm,
Rabbi Jack
ushered her
into grief.

On the way out, we stepped from our cars
to wash our hands.
The world had returned to its ordinariness.
Telling jokes, the barrel-armed gravediggers
resumed what we had started,
filling the hole with dirt.

Death is such a dirty job.
May the clean, invisible spirit
of sanctification
house them too,
and all their loved ones.

As I drove off I wondered:
whom have I hurt? Whom have I bragged to lately?
Who have I offended?
Whose hopes have I crushed?
I must say how wrong I was—must
admit: I am but clay He breathed into.

In the street outside my home,
I held my girlfriend close,
who had came out to meet me
under skies like Goya's Toledo,
and I thought:
I will not see you, dear,
very long here
before this kiss
is torn from our mouths.
Let me hold you,
as though for the last time,
while now we are here.

WHEN I WAS A SOLDIER

Sometimes I walk with my face and hands dirty
in San Francisco,
broke in the bright strange dream
of my manhood, and I remember
that I have done many things
in my life — the street,this day,
are not the last stop, and immediately
I cheer up, chide myself: *what am I down for?*
I have such incredible memories,
like of that time when I was
in the Israeli army crossing
the desert armored
in a personnel carrier
when suddenly the columns stopped

in a dust cloud,
wind blew back the scarf around my neck,
I squinted through goggles
as one by one the hatches flew
skyward and troops jumped free —
and by God when you see
your buddies
jumping out, jump too! —
I ran to where they were running,
churning sand to reach the commander
who stood powdered with dust, except
where goggles left
big owl rings around his eyes —
he faced a circle of the bravest,
finest soldiers imaginable,
and I elbowed my way through
to see what held them there.
It was a desert narcissus to be exact: very rare,
lilac-white, lithe and sad as a betrayed
woman slumped in an evening gown —
it grew on a remote plain, and had survived flood,
roaming camel hooves of mounted Bedouin,
the flowing passage of trampling herds;
had endured withering heat, scorpions
and jackals, and I guess that only
the beautiful angry love of God could have kept
the thing alive —
so, we laid down our firearms and unbuckled
our helmets and vests,
we shrugged off thousands of rounds of ammo
that we humped everywhere, and we put down
our sidearms too, everything, and melted to the
ground in a grimy
khaki-colored ring to observe the tiny fragile lady
cry all alone in the ballroom;
and distant jackals gathered on a hill,
stunned by the sun's bright fire, turning black —
and it's many years since then.
I am recalling this hungry-bellied on a sidewalk
in my new life reborn as a poet-
my soul does not starve:
it's such memories that keep me
going forward beyond where roads appear to end —

Hey Alan, I laugh, as my head nods off
and stomach rumbles,
Hey Alan, keep walking
and remember that time
when…

MONDAY AFTERNOON IN HAIGHT ASHBURY

You're in a sidewalk cafe
in Haight Ashbury, San Francisco
but unlike New York
your coffee cup isn't bussed
the minute you've drained it

They let you sit from morning
to night, undisturbed

Your cup refills
at the pace of your thirst

You can bag a big table
for yourself and sprawl

You can write poems
a single line in a day
or five pages
in one hour

You can read free alternative newspapers
go out back to the garden
to bake in the sun
or stare out the window
at the endless procession
of slackers

Or you can stare
at your hands
as you're doing now
thinking of the daughter
whom broken marriage
led you to abandon

She lives in Israel
with her mother

How, you wonder
without the bucks to send
a gift six thousand
miles away, will you fill
the void you've left
in her?

Or, you can take out
her picture, study it,
the one of her in profile
staring sadly through a window,

imagine that she is wondering
where you are
or you can visualize her waking
startled at night crying:
"Daddy!" But, you're not there

You're in Haight Ashbury,
in your thirties, recovering
from alcoholism, writing poems

You are like so many New Yorkers
who ran aground
in bars on bad marriage
hard labor, mindless consumerism

You made one last ditch geographic
to California to remake yourself
like a sixties movie hero
of mid-life crisis —

but it's the nineties so
you're dressed in black motorcycle
gear, not headband and sandals

and Tracey Chapman is teasing
tears from your eyes

When your forty
she'll be ten
and when you're fifty
she'll be twenty
and if you can live to sixty
with your booze-damaged
guts there'll be a reunion,
gifts, letters, phone calls,
sure, and even a book or two
dedicated to her

and maybe you'll
have dropped in one weekend and meeting
in the kitchen over a midnight glass
of milk, she'll tell you
that nothing you do or say makes it better
"You were gone," she'll say "I needed you then
I feel so empty"

You miss her cries of
glee, others reassure
her fears

there are times
when none but you
can help

but you do not hold her
you cannot hold her now
you will not soon fill your arms
with her softness, her blondness
her blue eyes, her face like yours

It is Monday afternoon
in Haight Ashbury
you are alone
and you say her name aloud

DAUCHAU

1.
In the gas chamber
I stood alone
in a strange kind
of silence
when suddenly
I heard a
roar of young male
German voices
& wandering
out saw
that nearby a
soccer match
was in progress

2.
As I walked away
I spotted a long hut, made of
wood,
something like a
big sauna
and thought that
perhaps it was the
groundskeeper's
residence and
strolled around to
the front where
I came face to
face with a crematorium

I stood
there shocked
then approached &
put my head into
the oven

NANCY REAGAN AND FRANK SINATRA

Did Frank cuff you to the bed
and keep his hat on while doing it?
And when it was over did he knot his tie,
cigarette dangling from his mouth,
smoke curling past a squint, and say:
"Don't worry. I'll be back. It ain't over
till the fat lady sings"
When he stopped answering your calls
and spotted you at concerts
disguised as a Mafia wife
did he dedicate the next song to you
and croon: I Did It My Way!
Did Ron ever know?
Or was he so consumed with
cutting back on social welfare
that nothing else mattered
anymore, not even you.

It must have been hell
to find him glued
every night to the T.V.,
obsessed with Panama versus
America, and Iranscam
playoffs.

Did you scream:
"Goddamit, Ron! I'm a woman!
Look at me, I'm beautiful!"
and grabbing a leopard skin
fur, rush downstairs to your
sportscar for a suicidal ride
on the wild side?
Did Ron follow in his Rolls,
force you off the road,
and smack you upside your head?
Did he shake you by the shoulders,
did your face bounce limp and crazy,
and then, did you melt in his arms,
press your cheek to his chest
and as he stroked your head, you gasped:
"Oh, Ron! I don't know what's wrong with me."

But it was Frank you were thinking of,
wasn't it?

Those blue eyes.
That arrogantly curled
Sicilian upper lip.
The shark skin suits and silk shirts.
You smelled the gutter on him,
and it drove you mad!
His Hairy proletarian buttocks!
His talk sprinkled with New York
cabby Yiddishisms, like Putz and Schmuck
and Bagel.
He even knew Black people!
Did he sometimes feel in your
arms like a homeless man
whose hungry suffering
made you cum like champaign?

Did Ron enter grim into the livingroom
one night, show you the used condom
he found under the bed while looking for
a sock, and ask: "What's this, Nancy?"
And you recognized Frank's brand:
Excita Fiesta, Assorted Colors, Ribbed.

Did he lurch with clenched fists
around the room screaming: "What's this,
Nancy, what's this?"
While you sat numb and stony
with the rubber in your hand squeezed
so hard that the last teaspoonful of
Frank's love spurted over your fingers
and you swore secretly never to wash it off.

When Ron calmed down, popped the Billy Graham
cassette into the VCR and asked you to go down
on your knees with him to pray for guidance,
was all you could think of the secret suppers
at Patty Minelli's Clam House in Hoboken,
where you could show a little
cleavage, and Frank lit your cigarettes.

THE TIME I DREW ANGELS

I once drew angels...
during my second marriage...
No, actually after the marriage was over,
when it was all in ruins.
After I had run off wth Rose
(My wife's best friend, and my best friend's wife)
and ruined that, as the war dragged into
its third year — the Lebanon War in '82; this was
in Israel and all us men were in the army. I was close to nervous
breakdown. My betrayed wife called, invited me to her place;
when I last saw her she broke a radio over my head. I had since
heard that she was threatening murder, had friends in the Israeli
underworld; for a time feared that she would have me hit — but, I
went to her home anyway. Why not? She had moved into a diingy
tenement neighborhood, a bleak slumlike project building, but she
was putting her life back together and looked better than she had
when I was shuttling back and forth between Rose's bed and the
army, and would spot her from a distance on a street, wearing dark
sunglasses and dragging home fishnet shopping bags filled with
bottles of cheap brandy — there were bottles
out on the table now when I came in. She cooked a lousy dinner,
bologna and eggs, some such crap. And the booze was out. With
her, dinner was just an excuse to drink, that's all, and we drank
now, as always. We were the ideal drinking mates. I had not even
minded very much — such good mates we were — when she
betrayed me with that cab driver one night; fucked him right in the
back seat while I sat upstairs iin the house, pouring myself
tumblers of brandy and I even brought them down two helpings —
but found them busy clasping white in a confusion of black lace
and tense thrusting buttocks, so I took the glasses back upstairs
and drank them both down — she unscrewed the cap
and poured me a glass now.
I was in bad shape. "You look terrible," she sad.
"I'm full of remorse," I saiid "I'm sick with what I've done."
She poured. She was silent. We sat and drank.
(And O.K., I'll own up. I was having a nervous breakdown then.
Period. Was even having paranoid delusions in my army unit:
imagined that my fellow soldiers, the best friends possible on
earth, the bravest kindest guys really, that they wanted to kill me
with a secret bullet to the base of the brain — crazy stuff like that)
"It's bad" I told her, "I'm having delusions."

She nodded. "Why don't you draw," she suggested, "draw how
you feel. My shrink strongly recommends it."
"O.K." I said.
She rose, returned with watercolors, set out paper.
I began to draw, and sipped from time to time from my glass.
She drew from the bottle straight. It was gold-colored
in the room and felt safe.
The pain between us actually formed a kind of embryonic womb,
enfolding and protecting us. We each had already hurt the other
too savagely to fear pain anymore. So, I drew. I drew
people with wings on their backs. I drew an angel. He had on a
news vendor's cap, and a poor man's sports jacket. He stared
toughly from the frame of the portrait. He looked gentle but tough
as nails. He was full of the heartbreak of his
love betrayals, full of the mercy that he felt for others. And it was
beautiful, it was located in a kind of nighttime Brooklyn with a
starry Van Gogh sky, and the angel's eyes were like both Bambi's
and Sylvester Stallone's, and they seemed to say that never again
on this earth for as long as the angel lives will the good or the
gentle people of the earth be murdered or shamed
or betrayed — And she liked my angels very much, she said.
It was the first and only time that I have ever drawn angels. It was
the last time that I was ever to see her too, because soon after, at
the height of the khamsin winds, she threw herself from a sixth
floor window
and was buried near Tel Aviv.

THE TWINKIE DEFENSE

Looking unwell,
Saturday morning Norman
Swings by
in his *BMW* with an elderly woman
chauferred on the passenger side—
his way of doing *mitzvot.*
As I hop into the back
His expert eyes of a retired dentist
snapshot my smile in the rearview mirror
and a shadow crosses his face—
Another cavity no doubt. He wants to fix my lousy teeth
but can't bring himself to work for less
then he once charged the actor Sidney Poitier.

Norman has no pity on unemployed poets, and so
this stalemate occupies our Shabbat
morning drives to *shul* — a pleasant dialectic
between high finance, dental hygeine and literary poverty
in which no point is ever reached
beyond that God dislikes us both.
Only, this morning, as I said, someone else
is in the car,
a Mrs. Goldstein who announces:
"I am Mrs. Goldstein!" but dosen't ask my name.
"Ninety years old, look at her!" Norman
grins.
"That's right!" Mrs. Goldstein
declares in a loud formal voice
"And my husband, Dr. Goldstein, may he
rest in peace was one of the best doctors
in San Francisco!"

Mrs. Goldstein wears a gold-embroidered pillbox
hat with a raised veil, dainty cream-colored
gloves and a splendid turquoise scarf. In
her ears shimmer galaxies of authentic diamonds.
She sits with shoulders squared, hands demurely
folded over a handbag with a clasp so golden that
a sunbeam bouncing like a laser off its polish makes
me squint, but she goes right on talking at a shout:
"Norman tells me you write"
"Yes," I begin, but she shoves my voice aside:
"Families tend to breed strains of occupation,
have you noticed? Some families breed writers
and other families produce lawyers. I come from
a family of lawyers, but married a doctor. So I have one
son who is a lawyer specializing in medical malpractice suits."
"And your other son?" I manage to interject.
She looks out the window, ignoring the question totally.
"I believe in a positive attitude," she goes on "and in taking good care
of the body. My husband was an allergist, you know."
"Oh" I say "I don't know"
"How long have you been in San Francisco?" she asks
icily.
"Three years"
"Well, that explains why you haven't heard
of my husband. Everyone in San Francisco

knows him. His research into the effects of sugar
on behavior was used by the defence of that man
who shot the Mayor some years ago…"
"You remember" barks Norman "That Milk guy.
Harvey Milk. Who shot Mayor Moscone!"
"Ohhhhhhhh" I nod "You mean the Twinkie Defence"
"Precisely" she says "The Twinkie Defence. "
"Where the guy ate so many Twinkies that
he became homicidal" says Norman.
"Yes" she says, lips pursed with pride "Exactly".
"Wow" is all I can think to say.
"Yes" she says, "it made quite a stir in this town, his theory."
"Well" I offer cheerfully " Pop a cupcake in my mouth
and Charles Manson at your service!"
"Oh, reaaaa-lly" oozes Mrs. Goldstein, her voice all
syruppy with distancing from the questionable taste
of my remark."
"Yeah" I chatter on "I completely lose it on sugar."
"That's because you're abnormal" barks Norman,
and turning to Mrs. Goldstein: "He's a poet. Life makes him nuts."
"And you" she shrills angrily at Norman "You're normal?
Why do you continue to eat so much sugar with that cancer
in your prostate?"

What's this?
Cancer? Norman? What a way
to announce
such a thing. These old folks are so
reckless!
My hand reaches
for my friend's shoulder. "Norman..."
But he shrugs if off.
Biting his lip, shouts, suddenly,
with uncharacteristic rage: "So what does it matter now
if I eat sugar or not? Who will care?" and reaching into his coat
pulls out chocolate and crams it into his mouth
as Mrs. Goldstein looks away
with unutterable disgust
and I stare
out the window,
shocked, at such an unrelenting
world.

ROSA

Rosa passes napkin-
wrapped wedges of honey
cake into my hands,
hurries about her kitchen
preparing
a 'snack'
to take the edge off
my hunger
A little chicken soup, a little
roast beef, a little carrot and raisin
salad, a little mashed potatoes,
a little challah, a little cake
'The biggest fridge in the
Sunset,' she boasts in her Czech
accent, 'stuffed with
food, no one goes hungry here,'
pressing a round tin cookie box
filled with breaded cutlets into
my hands
Then she peers anguished into my eyes
What does she see there? I dare
not know. I glance at the numbers
on her arm, tatooed at Auschwitz.
I want to say:
I am not Doctor Mengele, my dear.
I want to say: *the world has opened*
an abyss between us, that will not close.
Instead, I lean down to kiss her.
I peer as deeply into her eyes
as I can. It is time to be warm
and human, one creature
to another.

My brown eyes
contain just a hint
of Kafka's amicable terror
and Proust's poetic morbidity.
I am a nice man.
Her eyes ask no questions.
Where have you gone, Rosa?
How did they make you disappear?

I hug her, always, and sometimes I say:
'I love you,' to Rosa who is
nearly seventy, twice my age, and a
stranger, really, just a friend from shul,
she lives close by.
I don't even know
her last name.

FRANKFURT JEWISH CEMETARY

The flowershop proprietess
met my request
with lowered eyes
and from a draw removed the key
to the cemetary across the road.
Grateful, I bought an armfull
of her tulips as an irritated customer
checked his watch.
When the cash register bells
rang up the sale, I nodded to her
flower-scented suspicions;
said in Hebrew "Shalom"
and the door's bell tinkled
as I left.

Bells from local churches
thronged the air as I entered
the gate. My coat sleeve
passed over a spray-painted
swastica. Like praying
Jews with foreheads pressed
to the Temple Mount the de-
secrated stones for which no
graves could be found
leaned weeping in light against
a fence, and others, like seniors
fallen on winter streets, trembled
with broken hips. I took them into my
arms, lifted whom I could, kissed them.

I sprinkled their trampled lanes
with flowers, like salt over ice. I muttered

Kaddish, sang Ha'Tikva, stood dejected
and cried. But their silence could not be healed.
My own ghost followed me out.

And now it is night,
and I walk alone, unable to sleep
like one of the toppled stones
of Frankfurt Jewish cemetary,
a date of birth separated from
the fact of its death,
a visitor
to Germany come to cry
and snap
a picture.

AMEND

I make amends for your Hitler-scarred
crematorium womb
The SS shipped your uterus to
the miracle of birth that seemed
like a Nazi medical experiment,
left you blind for weeks,
unable to give suck
and loosed the ghosts of disease
from the Pandora's box
of your blitzkrieged pituitary gland,
and for years your eyes were a dark Dachau
In the barracks of your flesh your phobias wore boots
and whips hissed when you stood at the kitchen stove
dressed in old shoes like clogs
the limp housedress a striped prisoner's
pajama, and frantic over the steaming burial
pit of a pot of nutritious vegetables
to fortify the gallows of my health

Which gassed relative lurked
in the mashed potatoes?
Aunt Zelda, big fat complaining
seamstress who couldn't
swim and was torn apart by a guard
dog as she forded the river to escape?

Whose blood was that coursing
from my undone roast beef?
Must have been little Charlie's,
your cousin whose skull
was split by a truncheon
on the loading dock in Sobibor,
and brains crushed underfoot
by mothers
smuggling babies aboard

I was your forbidden animal child
of heaven smuggled unconcieved
to forests where you hid with
your stern-faced *bubbah*
in adolescent bloomers stitched
from gunny sack from crates of partisan
dynamite, and menstrual-spotted
as you cringed in chicken coops
and convents
of shrapnel-spitting dirt days and baying nights
of whistling bombs and human hunts
and somehow you survived , your body groaned
to womanhood, shaven-headed, head bowed,
shivering nude in campground subzero winter winds
of punishing guilt whistling through the barbed wire
of your American resettlement
to a Bronx flat
where you were monitored by police locks
and by two tall watchful lamps
like guardtowers
and where you wept with gall bladder & kidney stones
in your dim bedroom on *Sealy Posturepedic* mattress
Prisoner on a pallet of *Stella Doro* cookie crumbs
and dispensing advice to me
the young, new inmate of incarcerating
jackboot life,
and where it was dark,
very dark, no night to stay alone with you,
Poppa gone to work,
and your eyes shining dangerously bright

Drunk with hope of fostering
a child star

you had me stand
before your chair, holding
your hands, my eyes fixed obediently
on yours,
and told me to sing your favorite song
just one more time.
The belt in your lap made
sure I got it right
"Tea for two and two for tea,
me for you and you for me..."
and up leaped the belt
and down it struck like a snake,
and up again and down with a hiss
it bit
and oh I cried
no momma please
It bit my hand
I'll sing, I shrieked
I'll sing I'll sing
no momma please!
It bit my hand

I am sick in my head
from the Holocaust
since you were in the war
not me
you mustn't come in anymore
through
the door not
even thirty years before
to the little boy
with ear pressed to the door
of my pounding heart
whimpering: *please, go away*

Knock, knock, you knocked
And you entered cookie cut from shadow
but you mustn't come in anymore, Mom,
because in a man's heart everything
is intensely felt
like the screaming mouth my bones formed
when you snapped them,
and you must lay me down

in fire
and kiss me with iodine of sleep
but you still swear that you don't hate me
Of course you do
you hate me in your head
bright red
with the burst blood vessel of your face
You hate me in my blue suit
and Navy Oxford shoes
and don't care if I fall on my
face playing tag
You hate me from your three-legged chair
combing your broken hair,
whining from your warped mouth

You hate me for my breath
and for the beautiful Eden of pain
inside my head
I have gone inside there
skillful as a spider
and trapped you forever
in the silk of my endless ecstasy for fame
because my soul can stand more good
then you gave it credit for
My mind can bear more stimulation
then you bothered to exact
My flesh generates more love
then you were able to afford
And I promise to take good care of you
Of course, of course
I do
I promise not to die before you do
I promise not to die before
you do

IN A WINDOW DARK NIGHT

In a window dark night
a couple make love doggy-style
The squeaks of their bedsprings play
like mice in the dark trees
And then, with a fond pat

on her rump, her lover rolls himself
over: "Goodnight!", while she
crawls to the edge of the bed,
shamed, to pull a turtleneck
over her head

So she
lies awake pretending to sleep
as the dark furniture shapes
resemble elephants lumbering
away from a poisoned water hole
One of their number
has just horribly died
and he, her lover, is the poacher
who jumped from the bushes
with an axe to hack
off its tusks, even though
that poor elephant was still
alive, and she can see
quite clearly in the bedroom
how its eyes rolled back in anguish
that she confuses with her own

But it is an hour too late
for anything to make sense to anyone
The shape of her mouth is like
the white moan of the moon
and in her soul she knows
that it is best to keep still,
that one must sometimes
mercy kill a day the way
cowboys shoot the horses
they most love
when they are maimed,
and likewise, when you are maimed
then you must hold
a pillow firmly pressed against
the feeble struggles of your heart,
and pray and wait

I have waited a year to write this poem,
dear woman, whoever you are, ever since
I saw you that night in Frankfurt, Germany

as I passed your window
in the street and did not
mean to watch so long, but did,
transfixed by your degradation,
hating that man and wanting
to call out: "Take heart! Please!
Don't be ashamed!"
For like you I suffer from
a disease of infinite yearning
No colors bright enough
No feeling too strong
I never have enough of anything
And so live for less then I deserve

And I have counted every window
en route home to borrowed flats
thinking of you, in narrow streets
of strange, unforgiving cities,
as drunken lovers, arms about
shoulders, dance
with the shame of the past
to an unseen music
of secret fire

MY MOTHER DOESN'T KNOW WHO ALLEN GINSBERG IS

"Ginsberg" she asks by phone "Is that your friend from Israel?"
"He's a famous poet" I explain. "I've been invited with
him and Kathy Acker to a Jewish festival in Berlin."
"Acker" says my mother, her voice cross "This is a Jewish name?"

My Mother doesn't know
who Allen Ginsberg is.
She doesn't know who Anne
Waldman is, or Charles Bukowski.
My mother doesn't know that I make
a kind of living on stages
screaming my heart out
to strangers at five hundred dollars a pop,
and that there's some debate about whether
or not what I and others like me do should be considered

poetry. My mother was arrested by the *Gestapo* in 1942.
She was 12 then. She's 60 now. She lives in Florida,
where every so often a German tourist gets shot.
To my mother, that is poetry.

My mother doesn't like the idea of a Berlin
Jewish festival. She cannot understand what
Jews feel festive about over there.
"And what is this 'celebration' for?" she asks coldly.
And changes the subject before I can answer.
"So, what will you do there?" she asks "Give lectures?"
"We'll read our works" I say " talk in panel discussions."
"Talk?" she says "In English, I hope!"
My mother doesn't like the sound of German.
"It's a funny thing" she says "I see the tourists
on the beach, in their bathing suits... what could be more
harmless? But when I hear them speak I
imagine them in uniforms, and become afraid."
My mother sees Germans in bathing suits
transformed into Germans in uniform,
and my mother fears that having once
narrowly missed killing her they might yet succeed
in killing me. As a child in war she saw such things
as babies tossed through the air and shot.
"Like crying angels, they looked" she says.

My mother doesn't know who Allen Ginsberg is.
She watches German tourists sun themselves
on the shore. Sometimes they don uniforms
of German language, march to her condo,
call up through the intercom and order
her downstairs with one suitcase con-
taining 6 kilos of clothing, and food
for a journey of three days.

My mother doesn't know who
Allen Ginsberg is
and I wonder if she knows who
Alan Kaufman is
She can't understand
why any Jew would ever
want to go to Germany

My mother doesn't know who Allen
Ginsberg is
she looks older than her years
but younger than the death she
still manages to escape
in retirement on the beaches
of Florida where there are not too many
round-ups for the camps, and one is safe,
generally speaking, if one stays indoors,
pretends not to be a Jew, even
to other Jews

My mother doesn't know
who Allen Ginsberg is
She has tended to regard most
'high' culture
as a kind of Disneyworld
for intelligent people —
to her, the 3 bolt locks
on her door are more important
than the collected works of Shakespeare
She knows that she's supposed
to appreciate books and pretends
to but my mother doesn't know who
Norman Mailer is, she doesn't know who
Maya Angelou is, she doesn't know who
wrote *On The Road or Leaves Of Grass or The
Awful Rowing Towards God*
She has seen six million of the best minds
of her generation gassed and burned

She is making baked fish
in the oven tonight, regardless of what
my father says about the smell
and, tossing a nice salad,
she goes into the livingroom, sets down
the meal on the T.V. tray, and as she eats,
stares through the big plate glass
window filled with night, measuring the
distance between herself and the sprawling,
creeping lights out there, humming the
Kaddish in her throat, the prayer for the dead,
for so many, many illusions dressed as life.

PART THREE: Rant

I KNOW HOW IT FEELS

My parakeet is trying to kill himself
He pops his head through the rungs of his ladder
and tries to twist off his head
Then he climbs to the top of the cage,
hangs upside down, and lets go
He pops up, weaves on his feet, dazed,
then inserts his head again in the ladder,
like a soda bottle cap,
and tries to flip off his head.
Then he climbs to the roof of the cage
and hangs dutifully upside down
and falls and crashes.
Then he climbs to his feet
and weaves around,
as I watch all this from the sofa,
wondering
if it's the thought of spending the rest
of his life with me in this little room
in the Lower Haight that is driving him
to such desperate lengths
Jeezuz, it could be, it could be...
I know how it feels to wake up
in this room's sad furnishings
and realize that there's little more to do
today than dress, eat
and stare at the wall without a hope
of getting out of this shit somehow.
I mean, writing poetry on welfare
is a lousy occupation.
And all you can write about
in the end is about writing
poetry on welfare.
Sometimes it occurs to me that
as a favor to us both
I simply should reach in and snap his neck.
I'm sure he would be grateful.
It's so hard to kill yourself when you're a bird.
Your wings are for flight, not suicide.

It is sometimes necessary to act with
unforgivable cruelty

as the only way free of the illusion
that you are free.
If I killed my bird, I would know
for once and all what
a complete asshole I am,
and what a relief that would be!
I could then head out
the door, unafraid to make the kind
of mistakes that make us laugh
The brand of mistake that gives us light in the dark
Such mistakes as ease our pain
through the long
uninterrupted
scream.

THE LAST EMPHYSEMA GASP OF THE MARLBORO MAN

I'M IN THAT LAST PHASE OF NICOTINE WITHDRAWAL
I can't sleep and have weird dreams
I woke up last night dressed in a white nightgown
There was a commotion at the window
I peeked out Saw David Lerner a poet on my fire escape
Apparently attempting to get in
Across the way a swat team of cops had M-16s trained on
his head and a police captain in a baseball cap shouted
through a megaphone: "Get off that fire escape!"
And Lerner who is two hundred and seventy pounds of angry
shag with tortoise shell glasses and an ax murderer's
wandering eye growled back: "Go fuck yourselves! I'm here
to kill for poetry" and I could see
his point/Since I've stopped smoking I can't concentrate;
woke up just before, feeling desolate
Came to the typewriter sat down to try to write this poem/So,
I might as well tell you the rest: I want to fuck everything in
sight/have unbelievable energy/now regard fucking as
some do smoking: am prepared to have sex fifty times an
hour for twenty four hours a day in every position known to
human kind. I am even prepared to fuck David Lerner if that
will stop me from smoking!!

Yeah, I'm working a good program: Have already made

amends to the children of two of my neighbors for the
baseball bat bludgeoning of their dogs; promise to replace the
old woman's arm with a prosthesis as soon as I can afford
one/and as recommended in the stop smoking handbook I go
to lots of museums — treat myself nice — do things I've never
done before — I went to the Picasso exhibit, stood before his
painting Mademoiselles D'Avignon and when no one was
looking called up a big gob of phlegm — all that mucus
breaking up inside — and spat it right into one of the
mademoiselles' cubist eyes. It was great! I then ran out of the
museum into the park knocked down a hot dog vendor and
positioning myself on the banks of the pond picked off
passing ducks with rocks: I killed several
I treat myself nicely now
I've given myself a great gift
I don't smoke anymore
There's other things I do
I dismember hamsters
I gorge myself on Captain Crunch
I've got contact with a Higher Power
I'm living the spiritual life
My face is out there for everyone to see
No more hiding behind that smoke cloud
I'm making gratitude lists: thank you for my new proficiency
with home repairs — The other day the toilet got
blocked up with too much paper so
I took an ax to the bathroom mirror
knocked open the drainpipe and as the shit-covered paper
flowed out over the floor, I got the roommate
responsible and wiped his face in it and now when he
hears a flush he sighs with loud relief and I laugh good-
natured as Joseph Stalin and say: "Remembering that little
nose-rubbing, huh? Ha, ha!" Also lately I've taken to
punching out windows around my neighborhood with a
screwdriver/ground floor stuff mainly
Once, I didn't look before I stabbed and sank the blade
to the hilt in the socket of this young kid's face that
was leaning out of a window but I got away in time
and the urge to smoke left me completely!
I fell to my knees on the steps of a church and thanked God
for lifting the imperious compulsion and now I know there's
more fun things than cigarettes out there like rape and war
and racism and I'm never lighting up again though I may

burn a few crosses to get by/I may register to vote for the
Republicans but at least my lungs are pink and my breath
smells fresh and look at the bright smile I crack!
It's great the girls love it when I chat them up
with the suave knowingness of a Ted Bundy/and I'm leaving
their bodies in ravines/I'm rolling them into unmarked graves
in southwestern deserts/Yes, I've bought me a car I'm learning
to drive at last/and I'm barreling down the road with shot gun
chainsaw garrote instruments of torture because I'm goin' out
there to maim, not smoke I could white-knuckle it but this is
what my Higher Power planned for me: kidnap murder and
torture bunker fun
So I've bought me an inconspicuous Dodge dart
with beat peace symbol seat coverings
And wear cut-off denims with a Born To Be Free
decal and tattered American flag and I'm out there
ready to be whatever people want me to be
A Merry drifter, a charming young guy on the bum
but most of all I'm smoke-free on Route 66
Because I've thrown away my coffin nails
Instead I'm picking off whatever gets my goat
in the landscape/and that's lots of things
I'm pouncing on my resentments with a vengeance
I'm pulling the fly wings off America
I'm bottling my sex urge in a specimen jar
I'm holding my childhood captive
in the cellar of depravity
I'm mixing my maypo with blood
I'm eating my Cocoa Pops
from scoured skulls
I'm boiling head soup on a Sterno stove
along the fabulous American road
and it's so beautiful I want to cry,
with a headless armless legless torso
comfortingly buried just a few feet away in a fresh grave all
happy, and me squatting here eating brains
under the Kerouac sky, a smokeless hipster a recovering
smoker and letting those feelings I once tried to stuff with a
Newport or a Camel,
letting those stuffed feelings erupt
like a geyser of blood from a butchered neck,
just letting them flow out as they come and not trying to stuff
them or anything

because I'm powerless
but just letting them flow out
of me and all over the bound and gagged
bodies of my fellow nicotine addicts
because I'm killing the smokers now
I'm ridding the earth of hopeless
tobacco fiends
I realize that as long as a single smoker
is left alive I will want to smoke
because they are the toxic relationships
Bradshaw talks about
they reinforce my low self-esteem
which causes me to smoke in the first place
and being powerless to change that
I'm killing them off one by one
in Mississippi in Texas in Minnesota
in those little towns where you find them perched
like lovers in a Salem cigarettes ad
against Kentucky horse farm fences
with unblemished lips and cherry lips
and a wanton gleam of smokers numbed lust
twinkling in their eyes and it's the eyes I go for first with an
icepick/It's the eyes I show them first — one eye to the other —
then the finger one by one/It's the toes then and the ears and
the nose until I hit smoker's
hole-mouth and stuff it with
twenty cigarettes and leave it like a totem on the sacred
smoking grounds of Philip Morris America, souvenir
of my spiritual growth!

UNTITLED #4

I still cannot smell after twenty years
of smoking. The machinery of my nose
is badly damaged.
It used to be so wonderful to smell.
As a kid I could smell my hand.
Now, I can't. Or the curtains. Or the flowers.
But the other day I cracked open
a brand new book and the sour odor
coming off the leaves
was like the smell of Tolstoy's breath.

I DON'T WANT TO BE WITH WOMAN

1.

I LULLABIED WITH LIES!
I talked a good show!
in motels and transient hotels!
on verminous mattresses!
kept up backyard
gardens in my head!
crazy cozy little homes
of my lust to get laid!
I fucked them into my dreams
with verbal displays!
I hung curtains with my cock
talked autumn in Paris
summers in Rome
sons and fishing poles
picnics and Honda Civics
With my tongue between their legs!
I promised cocktail parties,
life insurance
museum tours
and featherdowns
Everything I thought
a woman could ever want
(a fifties musical happy
ending movie of love)
and to cap it off
retirement on Golden Pond!
and one after another
I watched me
break their hearts
with a raging mouth
of landlord-beaten doors,
phones shut down
and food run out!
I storm-trooped
as they sat
at the edge of the bed
with tears down their faces
clutching their hands

trying to retain composure
while the bombs of my insults
fell like the ravaging of Guernica,
the horses of their pride
reared heads and neighed
screams of dying love,
the skeletal jaws
of their trust yawned
with teeth of trampled caresses,
and when only gutted Maidenforms
were left, they packed up their books
and dresses, Levi jeans and poems,
and left with tired hearts
to pursue their phantom princes.

Now, I don't want to be with woman.
I don't want to cry in their sex
and smile at their pain.
I don't want to kill the mother
in them who is killing me.
I cannot heal the shame of love.
I can only fuck like a man
and love like a boy
because this is what I have
learned to do.
It is what I know.

2.

I am sorry if you loved me.
I don't want to see your eyes
go cold at the end,
when the bedroom of our hope
becomes dreary as London.
I don't want to turn
my back in our winter bed.
All the love we made
in that bed is now a child
named Survival,
rejoicing in the rubble birds
of this morning.

I am looking out from
the porch where we embraced,

watching the sun rise
over Haight Ashbury.
The sun also rises
when love is dead.
It trembles with a quiet, silent light.
And I see that my grief is a child
trapped in the gross decay of my adult.
I ask: what power on earth
can call to health
a mind so steeped in its mistakes?
For, after a time,
you are what you've become,
doomed to die
of the cold inside,
and all the tattered dolls
and rattles decrepit
with time.

My afflicted mind of light
stares from its crib
with the hard finality of bones.
And I ask: what power on earth
can stop the gun
in my head
from going off?

ANONYMOUS

People would ask:
Why don't you write
about your feelings?
But I don't have any
I'd say, I drove
the little bastards
out.

They made lousy tenants.
They left their garbage
in the halls and argued
with each other through
the windows of my soul.
They were all fat

and working class.

I paid a torch
to gut the tenement.
They were jumping
off of ledges to escape
the smoke and heat.
My brain
became a den for
every kind of dope.

For a month now
I've been kicking,
and the feelings coming
down made me raise my
hand the other day in
rehab and say: My feelings
have come back. I'm
scared."

I'm raising my hand now.
I'm qualifying here, in
this poetry reading, this
church of human frailty:
years ago, I gave myself
like a virgin to emotion
and the asshole bit my neck.

I binged for years,
a cannibal vampire,
on coldness.

But today, without some trust,
I'll die unknown to myself.
I pray my feelings forgive me
for all their homeless nights.
The graveyard made them
hard.
For all I know, they've gone
to ex-cons, with angry
tattoos on their arms.

For all I know,
after the burn-out
they worked me
like a street
suckering strays
through lonesome
doors.

For all I know,
they joyrided my heart
into walls
and stripped my hopes
like hubcaps
and threw the spare
parts down a hole.

Because, as I get behind
my sobriety, and start
the engine up,
my courage sputters,
my dreams are low on gas,
and fate, like some
dumb punk,
had punctured
my good years.

ALIEN

There was never enough to eat
so I cut my father open
and ate what he kept in his belly
I ate Cadillacs and swimming pools
cusinarts golfclubs VCRs
The whole platform of the Republican Party
Wall Street column by column
The used trading tickets on the Bourse floor
I ate Mayoral speeches, candidate's wives,
the pigeon-shit spattered statues of the great shadowy
American cathedral
where homeless hunchbacks with imploding eyes
and ragged self-esteems feed their quaint hungers

on cupcakes and fortified wine
Some with crying infants dying in their arms
Bruised with nightsticks/not extras
in old Charles Laughton films
or bell-ringing peasants
of Kevin Costner Robin Hood
Hollywood imagination
but the human penis and vagina of desire,
the real feel that is over there in you
that I do not feel

So I switched off the television of reality
and went shopping in the sensurround
department store
where your homeless stench can't reach
I spent the day browsing
in all the clothes you'll never wear
wondering at the lucky ghosts
who might purchase them
Prowled near the changing rooms
hoping for a peek of washed, fed skin
Anything but to be outside
watching as the business crowds step
around you like so much shit, my brother, my sister

Kites drift past bright red
in the hot sky
and circling birds like a high school band
formation of brass wings
bring news of worldwide global war
while down below
you are a single starvation
growing forgotten
on the tiles
of Civic Center Plaza
Since
there was not enough to eat in America
or anywhere to sleep
and you took the the back alleys
to shit and dream
away from nightsticks
hoping that some alien might land
his ship nearby and take you away

And I guess you are the thrown-out child,
the bad kid who fucked up
in the eyes of the parent state
and got to stand in a corner
of the city night for a couple of years
with the dunce cap of hunger on your head
and what can I say   I got a home
I got what to eat
I got clothes
I got friends, I got T.V.

What happened how'd you slip out the door
down the stairs into the street to the park bench
of no return
Who threw you out of the lamps pool of light
from the night table the ashtray
the quart bottle of scotch
and line of coke
and cable porn
that lullabies American nightmare
to sleep each night?

I'm breaking from the past
and struggling for the future
and I'm wondering what's best
for the U.S. Vacuum Cleaner
The timing of the sell-off is crucial
Set up shop on Ritz Drive
Bring beauty to a pampered beast
With the economy in doldrums
all business decisions should be this easy:
Fire! and Fire! and Fire!
Memos in the rain
A graveyard of desks
I always said we'd be dead if we didn't have differences
Financial capital overwhelming human capital
A huge living excavation dust heap of money
There's a revolt brewing and there's gonna be walls falling down
Organized mythic aura exploits
Inciting riots using explosives
Grin lies, cold eyes and calculating
I am unwittingly the prime exhibit

If current events are negative I mark a curious detour
A man who hates secrets still harboring paranoia
My wild past more lonely than lonesome
Forlorn and nearly forgotten
I'm breaking from the past
and struggling for the future
I care about safety when trouble happens
The big story is even bigger than it seems
There is barely room in my mind for
the dreaded octopus shrunk and beheaded
Life is vanishing into thin air
I'm being turned inside out at a dizzying pace
A monolithic revolution improvised on a grand scale
I fight for my right to succeed
I'm breaking from the past
I'm struggling for the future
And I'm wondering what's best
for the U.S. Vacuum Cleaner
Independance was declared on Saturday
and lost on Sunday
Calls for resignation and uncontrolled disintegration
I am prepared, I want, to go all the way
A splintering of authority
The acronyms are hardly euphoric or politic
The club of crippled nations
The more external ties I have when the internal
pressure finally blows
the better the chance that my anguish will be dislodged
Because the end of meaning brings complications
for the winner
And I have won the poor dictatorship of my own
disruptive consequences
Breaking down at home
The phantasmagoria overloaded circuits
It won't be as spectacular as the dominating news
Accelerate the transformation
Last explosive advance happening as shock
To end up partly stressed a slave
Autarky and isolation are no longer an option
when you're on the breadline!

SHE

… binds me to the four poster bed,
mounts me shyly, awkwardly
my view of her is straight up, dwarfed at the foot
of her Colossus and reaching into
herself with a finger she balances to my lips
a drop of wetness on a fingerprint,
like a specimen on a slide, inserts, and roughly
massages my tongue and teeth
as if to say: *You have tasted me before*
but never against your wish, helplessly
regardless of what you want.
And it is good for me just now
not to know whether or not you
want to. I am free to predominate over you,
as a fact of life, like water or air, unavoidably alive
indisputably so, like the taste in your mouth
of a food that you once ate but cannot remember
the name of, like a medicine when you are
chained to your bed by a fever of the soul
or the foul broth given on Devil's Island
to the prisoner of solitary
confinement
who broke the rules,
must be punished,
say, for jerking off
or having sex with another inmate
or the time that you played
with yourself in the bathroom
of your mother's house
as she shouted and pounded
on the door, enraged
ordering you out,
perhaps to be shot
for the crime of having sex
with your own
lonliness

She empties into me a solitude that says:
When you touch me you don't want to
So I'll bind you and you will…
but she can't believe my touch

My hands are trapped. I can't touch her
She believes only in what she cannot feel
Only that is real to her
The woman is my lover, and I love her
Grateful, I drink
from the cup of her
unrepentant selfishness

Then she pours her
solitude into me
as climaxing moans
fill the room like ghosts

JAVA MAN

In a cocaine Mercedes
In a Giorgio Armani
and the endless
fly shit
of the slums
encrusting
your upper lip
like a black mustache
you're shipping out that fresh-roasted
that decaffeinated
and that deep aroma
hysterically good to
the last drop in your mouth
is how you blow
your brains
out in a manic fit
of anxiety
because you've got that Catskill
stand-up comic edge
that Lenny Bruce
New York fuck you
angry look
You've got that talent for
urinal jokes
and for kinky sex
You've got a talk radio
call-in host big mouth on

that ends badly in brothels
with dead naked girls
dangling slashed throats
over four poster beds
as the Mafia pimp
nuzzles your dropped
jaw with a silencer
and the straight edge razor
drops from your hand
and you don't even know
how you got here....?

It's that coffee, man!
It's that caffeine buzz!
You're ahead of the race
of the human marathon
your necktie in the wind
and patent leather kicking
like a motherfucker
up the corporate career track
as the IRS cheers you on
in the Republican decathlon
of economic disaster
because you're a gold medalist
of greed, and the secret of your
success is twenty cups a day
on a sour stomach
indigested
like Napoleon's
by two pounds of coffee
grounds cancer
You eat and shit drip filters
and the eyes bulging from
your head have been smashed
with a monkey wrench,
mistaken several times
by punks for headlights
and who needs a bathroom anymore?!
Now, you just do it in your
pants or wet your girlfriend's bed,
because you can't hold it in
Charlie Parker, you've zipped
the jazz wine of caffeine bop

scatting your bladder
and you're looking to relocate
permanently to a bathroom,
preferably one with a view
in New Mexico
where you can bash your head
through a neighbor's plate glass
porch door
with a friendly grin, like Juan
Valdez, and to sing: Ooooopa,
oooopa, ooooopa! A little more coffee, pleeze!
And Goooopa, goooopa, goooopa!
A little more Java, jeez!
A little rapid eye movement cup of Turkish
would be nice, a little bit of Maxwell House,
a double latte cluster bomb,
a cappacino hand grenade exploding in your skull,
a gas pedal floored in a goofy race
to the cliff's edge of your shot nerves,
and singing: Ooooooopa! Ooooooopa! Ooooooopa!
A little more coffee, please. And goooopa,
goooopa, gooooopa!
A little more java, JEEZ!

CHOW DOWN POEM FOOD

I want to get laid, so I might as well eat. But what will I eat today?
My stomach is overhanging my belt like a tongue with a drooling belly button/ I want to eat a Whopper raw, crack open a pack of Oreo's/pour sauce down my throat straight from the pan, wolf down mashed potatoes
Yeah, I like that word: *wolf*. Also, the expression:
scarf, as in: scarf down three steaks.
And these days I've noticed a new waddle in my step/ Tip the scales at three hundred pounds and climbing
I've used up the notches in my belt
My sports jacket's tight under the pits
I can't walk out of stores with clothes no more
Instead, now the tailor regards me with cold, clinical eyes of disgust, like a doctor, and says in a curt voice: "Step up here", and leads me to a small scaffolding before a mirror, and loops a tape measure around my torso like a noose, and hangs my waistline from the belt until dead.

Holy Goodyear blimp Batman! I've gotten fat!
When I go to the zoo in my Bermuda shorts and plod past cages
lapping at ices I hear the lions snort: "What a beast!"
I'm what tourists now go to see! I can't cage my appetite!
Hey, I'm food-abusing! I'm on a fast food spree!
I'll ***have:*** three big Macs, two whoppers with cheese, one super burrito, one chicken burrito, four tortillas, two extra large servings of fries, a fish sandwich, three cherry pies, and a part time high school age slave
labor worker from an oppressed third world country, sandwiched between two juicy sesame seed buns with special hot sauce and a cherry tomato popped into her mouth, and don't forget the napkins and straw!
Yeah,
I'm orally fixated; can't stop thinking of food.
I use to like having sex and going to movies
and things like that!
Now, I just want to lie in bed nibbling Stella Doro breakfast treats
and snackin' on Gerber vanilla custard baby foods
Gosh, I'm jones'n for Tapioca!
I live at the sizzler!
I've got a shrimp tail growing out of my ass!
My hero is Hoss Cartwright!
Pass the peas pass the butter pass the rolls pass the ketchup
pass the roast beef pass the homeless pass the grits pass the congress pass the string beans pass the breadline pass the junta pass the diamonds
pass the oil pass the dead baby pass the bayonet pass the burning cross dead jew black puerto rican hot dogs barbecue sauce
Hey, I'm **h u n g r y!** Take my order!
Let's go to the Third World supermarket and buy up a few countries worth of natural resources and eat that shit down and hey, I'm still hungry!
Lets jump in the car and go to the big mens shop and the large womens department and buy a few pairs of briefs made from circus tents and bras
stitched from parachutes and commando jump over troubled parts of our country and squash the poor to death!
Hey, I'm getting big as a house and I like it!
I'm Mother Goose, only, instead of a shoe I live up my own ass!
And make sausage from my spleen!
Try it, you'll like it!
Because I'm the behemoth of American appetite
and I'm comin to your town soon,
a Pillsbury doughboy out of control
in an ss republican party fascist uniform
lookin to set up shop as human beef manufacturer
hey I'm comin to make chopped meat out of you

I'm grindin up that garlic and that paprika
and greasin up the frying pan with hate
and I'm gonna pop you in there one vote at a time
because I'm hungry for human food
I'm a government of by and for Jeffrey Dahmer
A genocidal cannibal kind of guy
With hefty chompers and thunder thighs of Texas good
old boy rollickin political picnics, cutting deals with
the chicken breasts and corn cobs
and polyunsaturates of clogged financial arteries
and genocidal foreign policies
And when the universe spreads its big cheeks
with a sky-rumbling lightening jagged crack
of ominous ass and the gas clouds of cosmic indigestion rumble
with atomic war, or more likely the economic ruin of an overboiled
spaghetti-insufficient roughage diet,
with a Brooklyn cheer, an audible raspberry, I will be born
A fart In The Dark New American
swelling the savage belly of life with a tongue thrust from inflated cheek pouches and eyes popped enthusiastic
and a long, loud trickle of bppppppppppppph! erupting uninterrupted from the clapped together half-moons mighty clashing cymbals of my posterior,
with my eyes squeezed shut in transcendental American trance
Inscrutable milk-product of a non-dairy meat-based culture
A yogurt virus in the beef plant of sloppy glistening glyceridic gunk stuck to the blood-soaked meat packing plant workers' rubber yellow Wellington boots/ Though in the end its all gristle ain't it?
The mothers milk and the calf boiled in it
The harrowing slaughter of anything tender
and the dull deadly torture of our own offspring
To be boiled alive in mothers breast milk
A big Mac and milk shake to go
An egg salad with mayo on rye
A Ronald Reagan on David Dukes with
a side order of Newt Gingrich
America, cosmic kosherization might help you
but you want to kill your Jews!
America, only soul can save you but
you want to kill your Blacks!
America, you're your own face
reddening with rage
And pretty soon I guess you'll put on the uniform
and hop out on one leg thrust into a jackboot,

the other barefoot, a kind of Herman Goering Jackie Gleason
ready to pow zoom batter the Alice wife of your love
into a gas chamber, and whip the defecating Norton naked kids
of thrown bodies into pits,
and tattoo the Trixie forearms of muu muu Brooklyn
for a handful of ash! O, mourn fat man fascist.
What are you crazy, or what?

I'm throwing up on you now, regurgitating your robbed soul
Down on my knees in the racetrack jockey stalls as pure puke
of Buchenwaldian war rooms and oval offices
My weight jumped to four hundred plus
as I ride astride the skeletal nag
of apocalypse
whipping its bony flanks down the last stretch
of human skulls-paved track
and toga wrapped Americans cheer me on to the new Rome.
Yeah, I'm pounding that stretch hooves spitting dirt
past nuclear submarine hoagie-infested coastal
cancerous sparkling reefs fluorescent
with atomic spill, and sunrays diarrhetic
splatting through the ozone toilet hole,
and billions of dolphins cods mermaids
roiling the waves belly up dead tuna
and no shrimp cocktail for us folks no more,
and the next thing to go is blind beef don't ya know
pampas-broiled Argentina style
on the death squad plains of the pampas-sero,
and veal calf babies sledgehammered
skulls crushed
on the congress floor
they eat brains raw
and the next thing to go
is them vegetables
biogenetical malformed death spinach
from labs CIA
and then the FBI cracks down on racially
impure juice orange
and also finally thank god
on turnips not of white christian origin,
and the only good american, I say, is a fat american
layered blubber belly wheelbarrowed
lumbering in a beet sugar

daze through the cholesterol inferno
And I think that by eating all this food
I don't have to believe in life,
and I think that by eating all this food
I don't have to help the poor,
and I think that by eating all this food
I can really hate myself, and you, and
be the big mountain me beef stew moron
that I think of myself
dressed in newborn blue pink
and waiting like a trapped caveman to thaw
out of my glacier of civilization rampage
with fat dollop tears of joy down my brainless dreamless face
and a Barney Rubble baseball bat
brain bashing its way to Armageddon
through Gazan suburbs of corpulence
with an ice cream cone stuck unicorn in the middle
of my forehead,
because Ronald MacDonald *is* Jesus Christ!

RELATIONSHIT

I'm in a relationshit! Hey, it's great!
At night with undying love we ball!
Come morning she falls from bed griping: "Crap! Fuck! Didn't wear the diaphragm! We both get so depressed that we can't get to work! Just lie all day with wasted looks, asking each other back and forth: Do you think I'll get fired for not going in? And of course, the answer is: No way! Not when you're in a relationshit! Because even though this is our eighth missed day of work this month (and there's only been eight days so far) and even though we don't even bother to call in sick, we just don't show, when she asks me if I think she's pregnant, I lie and say: Hell no! because I've been down this road before and can already imagine abortion clinic and a right-to-life picket sign smashed over my head, because there's a demonstration going on, the nation expressing itself in bedrooms across America, as a right-wing Freudian cop wacks my knees with a psychic nightstick! OW! while my girlfriend stabs a priest to death in dreams of the Midwest, yikes!, using a nail file from her moist, angry purse, and next she's on her back on a table under hot lights ankles in stirrups, riding her pale horse of loss into liberation as a pale frog-faced crack fiend unlicensed gynecologist with wrinkled thumbs from the rodeo burbs scrapes her womb with a tongue depressor left over from an old Good Humor Bar and I'm fathering back alley murder because the supreme

court got its way! Hey, I'm having a relationshit! I love her so much! I can't bear to use a condom! Love is a life and death affair!
I'm in it for sex not latex!
I like my taste of skin!

And for a permanent washing machine mortgage on the life insurance monthly premium of our inevitable divorce, we're destroying our souls and ruining our lives! We've killed off our parents! Fired our bosses! Hurt all our friends with snarls of Campbell Soup contempt! We're filling up the emptied cans of ourselves with Microwaveable jealousy bombs that threaten to detonate hamburger-slaps and French fry shrieks!
Hey , look, we're draining that willpower! We're sinking survival! We're driving each other nuts with old boyfriends and new girlfriends and lovers we didn't even know we had, parading them out there lurid before each other on the burlesque stage of our vanity, pretending that each night we get secret calls from Chippendale hunks or animated centerfolds, so that we can't even bear to take a shower scared that the other is on the bedroom phone with someone hungry for a piece of ass, some Frenchman or hairstylist who understands, and I can't even soap myself without shutting off the water and poking my head from the shower curtains to listen and what I hear is: O.K., after he leaves I'll meet you downstairs in a cafe, and then we'll come back up here and fuck our brains out!
Even though I'm the only one at home when I'm hearing this!
H E L P!
When was the last time I had
a good wash? Why, I can't remember!
My body stinks!
I don't even brush my teeth
because the loud scrape
of thistled down enamel drowns
her cheating whisperings on the telephone to lovers
who are all named Uncle Joe, she says
when I ask her, all Uncle Joe, aged 79,
but I don't believe her! because according to her answering machine messages
which I eavesdrop on
while she sleeps, she is having sex
with three different genders of six
different races, including a circus dog
who barks after the beep!
But I'm having that relationshit
no matter what!
I'm in an Ozzie and Harriet
mode of acceptance,

sitting with dick in hand
mumbling through hot tears:
"Oh bitch, I hate your
fucking guts!"
Because I'm a committed kinda person
I tried dating
It sucked
It costs too much money
No one puts out on the first date anymore
and I'm so broke by the second date
that if she agrees to a third date
I'll tie the knot with her
just for the free meal and flop
in a hotel her parents pay for
because when my choice is between
welfare and fetuccini, hey! And
I'm bored with my own life but
the great thing
is that I don't have to live
it anymore
I'll just live hers,
all ready-made with a complete set of new
problems for me to solve
So I'm eating her food
I'm wearing her clothes
and reading her books
and pretty soon I'll be ready
to take up her sex
and she'll take up mine
we'll get ourselves
pets and become the pets
I'll be a Chihuahua
She'll be a hamster
we'll go to the pet store
live there in cages
begging strangers to please
take us home
for use as substitute husbands and wives
and maybe Disney will make a movie about us
called The Sex Addicts
in which we're chasing each other like Tom and Jerry
around the livingroom
with murderous claws and meat cleavers

screaming I love you!
as we blacken our eyes with restraining orders
and annoyed neighbors pound the ceiling and walls
as porcelain smashes and the shattering lamps ignite
the curtains
because we're having a relationshit!
Procreating in the American image
Adams and Eves of Hollywood
New love kids on the unexplored shores
of the nineties
and no one gives a fuck if
we're Joel Steinberg and Hedda Nussbaum
POW's downed over our own livingroom
our shame-puffy faces stapled
to the television
a little foundling between us to murder
a little inner child to butcher
and we're going to adopt the little dear
right now, and we'll parent it, you'll see
just like we re-parented the little child in us
with Hostess Twinkies and handcuffs and loud smacks
in our condo torture chamber, listening to Bradshaw
on four poster low protein beds of sleep deprivation
and bandaged broken nose coitus
and there's more murdered children filling
up the closet of the national libido, but noone notices,
because this is America, and we're having a relationshit immersed in Jeffrey
Dahmer acid baths and hand saws and people mind their own business in this
country when they hear screams they figure we're in a band or something
with used diaper guitars and bloody MTV
on loud because we're in love
The Nat King Cole misty kind
here we are happy as two kittens in a jar
filled with phemaldehyde
and clawing for air at
the glass as our panicstricken
faces drown
unheard...

ANTHEM

Tonight, the naked backs
of this last generation
bend under the whistling
          torment straps
of drunken Republican Dads
as hydrogen unfolds
the screaming flowers
from our mouths —
So, I ask: what sort of world
shall we build
as our addicted flesh
feeds holes
in their
poltergeist golf course?

Are we human beings,
or are we little perforated
cells screaming to be fixed
to the trembling brim
with chemical substitutes
for God?

Shall we build a
Mom and Pop
American world
of tagged big toes
ziplocked in body bags?

How long can we stretch
this order of Big Mac
homeless folks to go
for the Kingdom of Hades?

Or will we break
free at last
of our tongue-tied,
tearful awkward
ugly adolescence
and rage goodbye
to the relentless
George and Barbie dolls

of our unmentionable sorrow
and for once and all
smash the plastic
trumpeting seraphim
crib mobile of Jingoism
filling our
newborn eyes
with old lies?!!

For what is the meaning
of this medicine wheel of crazy
but the wheel itself
wheeling through the cosmos,
fueled on blood,
its gaskets blown
by the Christianity
of Dull.

Why do we still slobber
at the tit of this government,
that killed our father,
enthroned a lover,
our lips stained
with shit, remorse
and tears.

Why are we still
money, money, money,
O, please stop
hitting me money?!

Who declared us dead,
who have yet to die,
and left us angels
on rubber sheets
of embryonic urine
to evolve freeze-dried
from seahorse to human
    imbecile,
and to pray on our
knees like mud-painted
paranoids,
peering through cave mouths

of destitution
at the property holdings
of IBM?

Who sent us hungry
to our room
with soap-washed mouth
to sting with first
insulted cheek
slapped by a masked
man dressed as a butcher,
and the walls
parting to reveal staircases
to televised heaven,
and the gray, cold-wrapped
skin of our bone hands
uncorking bottles
of fortified deportation
railroaded right into the gutter?

Who punished us
with fobs, springs and bells
from borrowed clocks
knelling in our skulls
poor poor poor
war war war
like wagons
claptrapping briskly
down the roads of time
when there are no roads or time
but only our trash-filled
skins hauling
to shelters,
in cities of murderous winter,
to lie with blankets slipped
from our shoulders,
begging for another portion
of existance,
getting none.

There comes the day of the
bottom line
when the four bookies

of Apocalypse
ride in on the horses
you've played and lost
When you have spoiled
everything you have ever touched,
when the lowest of pimps
despise you
and the worst sluts
straddle your hips
like a saddle,
and you don't care
who lives or dies
as the consequence
of your love,
or is ruined, or goes
to therapy,
or quits a job,
or moves away.

There comes a day
when you haven't a soul
or a brain
or a good heart
and good riddance
to those fucking parasites

When you are all
song, belly and prick.
laughter and memory
and hands

your sandled
feet sport painted nails
like drops of blood
on crucified toes

You dance lip to lip,
with entangled legs,
your heart impregnated
by a taste for justice

You bring only the necessities,
your wallets and purses empty

And
you will do nothing to destroy
America,
only everything and everyone in it

There comes a day
when like a child
you topple nations
with your laugh
When your brain
is mentally ill
with prayer
your face pockmarked
with the acne of truth
and since your thoughts,
really, are just feelings
in drag,
and you live in the gutter
on welfare,
and your insomnia is chattering
to nowhere non-stop
you can be spared
for a revolution —

Don't fear: you'll
        know it
when it comes.
With prayers born
of a people's rage
from the loaded
muzzle of a gun

America, shame
        is a great laugh!
America, George Adolf Hitler Reagen/Gingrich
        in your time!
America, brainwashed
gas chamber-exhausted cadaver skies!
America: one out of four
Afro-American males
slain or jailed
America, ruled by
dynasty of conspirators

America, men, women,
children and babies
gassed through their pores
in our wintry gutters

I love your name:
        America

It sounds like
hallowed faces hopeful
gape
over the ship's rail;
sounds like glimpsed
Statue of Liberty green
against the gray
sea...

like stone flame kept,
cold arm
upheld,
lighting the bronze gate
to urban cement
concentration camp

O, nation!
MAKE WHOLE.
HEAL.
I LOVE YOU.
DO NOT BE AFRAID.

Gorgeous America,
Bring out your dead!

STUD OF THE APOCALYPSE

We are the ships
of the human soul
stalking fear in a shadow gulf

We are the transparent suits
with black snouts
filtering gas launched to

kill the child in us

We are the last shamans,
the final seers, of the last
peace of the end days
of the bloody debacle
of history

We have seen all this before:
drilled under
school desks for bombs;
ordered the Time-
Life series of books
on the history of conflict

Have done as the ad proposed:
died with the troops at Dunkirk,
cried with the Marines
on Pork Chop Hill
and the Screaming Eagles at Tet

We fought with them side by side
in hand to hand
full-color photographic combat

We wept with them, we bled,
we prayed
in texts with captions,

and we received as bonus,
free and at no obligation,
a handsome designer faith
shaped like a NIKE sneaker.
And from our rearview mirrors
hung styrofoam dice
and plastic Madonnas

And on our noses rode visors
like robot eyes

and cigarettes plugged our mouths
and walkmans stopped our ears
and condoms sheathed our cocks

but for all these gods, luck, perfume,
narcotic music and venereal
precaution

we were immaculately infected
by the stud of Apocalypse
and we are in love
And our lover has many faces:

He is swarthy with a mustache
and for lunch gases Kurds

He is lean and wears glasses
and shoots golf with the Devil

He is an unshaven cobra
in a checkered head dress

A Serbian Eichmann
Prime Minister in drag

His are the perfect deltoids
of the steroid redemption

The wafer of the Shwartzeneger
termination

Boys and girls of every
creed and color die
in the democracy of his war

He is the full-blooded Angel
of Death, with a sword
such as any healthy
Christian, Muslim or Jew
can recognize

The winged Aryan of extinction
inured to pity, under contract
to hate,

the highest paid
athlete in Paradise,
striding the global charnel
house, hacking left
and right,

his massive biceps
rippling as he cleaves
the skull of a civilian

His prize winning triceps
like anvils as he
dismembers
a soldier

We are the audience
of the film house tomb
on the ticket cue
of the world movie

and one by one our tickets
are received at the gates,
torn,

and clutching stubs,
one by one we enter
the magic lantern mystery
of war,

and take our seats
in a tank, in a cockpit,
in a trench,

blindfolded
hostage at a key installation,
or in the ranks of the Congress
or in the pews of a church
or in the waiting of venereal
disease, and foreheads
marked with ash,
in a circle of embers,
we pray for death
to make an offer

And we know the souls
death in life

for which we dress
in black

Our tattoos stamp us
like a passport
at the point of no return.

Inside, we are
tired, angry, sick,
ashamed of flowers,

Our worst fears
have come true:
we will not see
the face of darkness.

Ignorant of what we've lost,
our poems will declare
that here lay
unholy bones of rage
which made no peace
with God.

And the worms,
who cannot read,
will eat
the artwork
of the flesh.

THE SADDEST MAN ON EARTH

The saddest man on Earth...

ignored how the rain felt
as he left home
for the last time

Wore down
his boot heels

searching for the woman
of his dreams
but never understood
that life is a woman

Lived in a town
where sadness was illegal
and where grinning
cops ticketed his face
so often
that he lost his license
to cry

The saddest man
on Earth
tuned guitars
but couldn't play them
cheated the IRS
of his own refund
fathered a child
who thought she saw
him in perfect strangers
yet didn't recognize
him face to face

I met him once
in a bar
toasting the mirror
with his stare
He had come
south to start
life over

He was a
Mozart of silence